The Restless Ilan Stavans

LATINO AND LATIN AMERICAN PROFILES

Frederick Luis Aldama, Editor

THE
RESTLESS
ILAN
STAVANS

OUTSIDER ON THE INSIDE

STEVEN G. KELLMAN

University of Pittsburgh Press

Published by the University of Pittsburgh Press, Pittsburgh, Pa., 15260

Copyright © 2019, University of Pittsburgh Press

All rights reserved

Manufactured in the United States of America

Printed on acid-free paper

10 9 8 7 6 5 4 3 2 1

Cataloging-in-Publication data is available from the Library of Congress

ISBN 13: 978-0-8229-6585-5

ISBN 10: 0-8229-6585-2

Cover photo: Courtesy Ilan Stavans

Cover design: Joel W. Coggins

CONTENTS

PREFACE

I'm not the first person who feels that it's the writer's true occupation to travel. In a certain sense, a writer is an exile, an outsider, always reporting on things, and it is part of his life to keep on the move. Travel is natural.

—James Salter (Hirsch 38)

It is hard to think of an active American critic who is more prolific, influential, and controversial than Ilan Stavans. A public intellectual who has made his mark not only through his plethora of books—some of them bestsellers—but also through radio, TV, film, theater, and lecture, he is the recipient of official honors from Massachusetts to Chile and China. He has been invited to speak from some of the most hallowed podiums, at venues such as the Library of Congress, Lincoln Center, and the Smithsonian Institution. Already in 2006, more than twenty books ago, one critic, David William Foster, concluded a review by proclaiming that "there can be no question that Stavans is now himself a cultural phenomenon" (Foster 74). That phenomenon has also been reviled as a dilettante and a charlatan. Though Stavans holds an endowed professorship at Amherst College, one of the most prestigious liberal arts institutions in the United States, he rarely misses an opportunity to taunt the academic mind.

Stavans grew up in Mexico City and, after his emigration to the United States in 1985, became a widely sought-after commentator on things Spanish, Latino, and Latin American, an insider with a talent for communicating with readers outside the Latino community, which, at 57 million and growing, has mushroomed into the largest ethnic minority in the United States. However, as a Mexican immigrant who did not grow up in East LA, El Paso, Spanish Harlem, or Little Havana, Stavans does not fit comfortably into the category of "Latino" and has often been resented as an outsider who presumes to speak for Latino—and, especially, Chicano—experience. Moreover, he grew up within an insular Jewish community in a country in which Jews are a tiny, harassed minority, further emphasizing his outsider status and undercutting his authority to speak even for Mexicans. "Do I feel nostalgia for Mexico?" he asks himself. "Not really, not fully. It was home while it lasted, but Mexican Jews never felt at home in it" (*Singer's Typewriter* 277). About Mexico, he says,

"The Jews are there, but the Jews are not of there" (Sokol 47). The 40,000 Jews of Mexico form such a negligible percentage of the total population of 140 million—that, as he notes, "few in this country of more than a hundred million will ever see a Jew in their entire lives" (*Return to Centro* 4). By contrast, New York, to which he emigrated, has a large Jewish population, but it is a heterogeneous metropolis in which everyone is both an outsider and an insider. "No matter where I live, no matter where I travel," Stavans explains, "the only place I feel I truly belong is New York" (Sokol 4). Yet, for 25 years, he has been living in western Massachusetts, more than 160 miles away from New York City.

Stavans has drawn on his background in Yiddish and Hebrew and his fascination with Jewish history and culture to write also about Jewish topics in ways that transcend the *mishpocha* to engage Gentiles as well. He has even published a Haggadah, albeit an unconventional one, a guide for conducting the Passover seder. At the same time, calling himself a "skeptic hedonist" (*Art and Anger* 4), he dismisses a belief in God as a "superstition" and insists that the foundation of religion is fear. Though lauded from the pulpits of synagogues and the podiums of Jewish book fairs, he berates American Jews, largely of Ashkenazi background, for their provincialism, monolingualism, and philistinism and has taken on the special mission of making them aware of Sephardi history and culture. He has made himself the principal patron of Jews—Ashkenazi as well as Sephardi—who write in Spanish.

Though Stavans characterizes Domingo F. Sarmiento's *Facundo* as "the byproduct of a quintessential insider parading as outsider" (Introduction to *Facundo* xvi), the formula could be applied to him in reverse: an outsider to Mexican, Jewish, and American cultures who offers insider insights about each. "Being an immigrant," he told an interviewer, "I cherish my role as an interloper. I look at American civilization from the outside in. And I'm no longer an insider in Mexico either" (Stavans and Yates 599). Throughout his work, Stavans brings a double consciousness—the nearsightedness and farsightedness of both an insider and an outsider—to Jewish as well as Latino themes. Of course, Latinos and Jews are themselves both outsiders and insiders within a society whose dynamic is both centrifugal and centripetal. Though still mistrusted and maligned, Latinos and Jews have woven their way into the porous fabric of American society to become industrialists, Supreme Court justices, movie stars, United States senators, professional athletes, and college presidents. Spanish and Yiddish terms and turns of phrase have been absorbed into standard English, and it is said that most Americans now choose salsa over ketchup, bagels over biscuits.

Furthermore, compounding his own double consciousness, Stavans has reveled in a kind of quadruple perspective. As outsider/insider to both of the cultures—Latino and Jewish—that claim and disclaim him, Stavans presents himself as a bridge between the two, the foremost commentator on Jewish Latinos, Latino Jews, and ties and tensions between the two communities. "I write in English for Americans about topics they know little about," he declared early in his career, "and I write in Spanish for Mexicans about topics they are unacquainted with. I act as a bridge, I symbolize dialogue" (Pakravan 51). Like James Salter, Stavans knows that writers are outsiders, and, like Salter, he embraces travel as a tonic alienating, defamiliarizing device; his book *Reclaiming Travel* begins by declaring: "We are creatures in motion, of motion" (Stavans and Ellison 1). But writing about those motions in some sense brings a writer back inside the community.

Language is not only Stavans's medium; it is his recurring theme. "To be obsessed with language is to be obsessed with the universe" (*Knowledge and Censorship* 103–4), he declares, obsessively. Proudly polyglot, Stavans is a translingual author who writes at times in English, at other times in Spanish. He also translates from each language to the other. As a critic, he is particularly drawn to fellow translinguals, including Felipe Alfau, Julia Alvarez, Hector Biancotti, Joseph Brodsky, Elias Canetti, Ariel Dorfman, Rosario Ferré, Albert Gerchunoff, Judith Ortiz Cofer, Fernando Pessoa, Richard Rodriguez, and George Steiner. His fascination with language in general is evident in his books on Hebrew and Spanglish and in *Dictionary Days* (2005), an account of his infatuation with lexicography. The premise that language shapes perception and identity is the starting point for much of Stavans's writing.

As the author or editor of more than one hundred books, Ilan Stavans has become a marketable brand and a valuable barometer to social developments in the late twentieth and early twenty-first centuries. Though a harsh critic of consumer culture, he has exploited it to his advantage, creating a recognizable and appealing voice that readers want to hear as it flits from the Bible to Latin jazz, to migrant farmworkers, to pornography, to the Inquisition, to *fútbol*. What Stavans has to say about Octavio Paz might be, in Princeton professor Rubén Gallo's phrase, "un ensayo literario que deslumbra por su soltura, elegancia y elocuencia" (Gallo 1037) (a literary essay that dazzles with its fluency, elegance, and eloquence), but it is, after all, just an essay, padded with wide margins and generous line spacing. Few bylines other than Stavans's would have induced a publisher to bring it out as an eighty-four-page, stand-alone book that a Canadian professor, Yvon Grenier, dismissed as "perfunctory, hollow, and unfocused" (Grenier 260).

Stavans's extraordinary productivity makes any attempt at writing a book about him doomed to imminent obsolescence. Between the moment that I write these words and the one in which they become available between hard covers, Stavans will likely have published half a dozen additional books. Any attempt to take the measure, midstream, of a torrent can at best be tentative and provisional. A book about Vladimir Nabokov published in the latter's fifty-seventh year, Stavans's approximate current age, could pore over such Russian masterworks as *Despair*

(1934), *Invitation to a Beheading* (1936), and *The Gift* (1938), but would have nothing to say about most of the glories of Nabokov's Anglophone phase, including *Pnin* (1957) and *Pale Fire* (1962); it might even be silent about *Lolita*, which did not appear in America until 1958.

Stavans prides himself on his interrogative rather than declarative—Talmudic rather than catechistic—style, his preference for Socrates and the wiser Talmudists over the dogmatists who put the Athenian gadfly to death. Unlike George Tesman, the academic careerist in Henrik Ibsen's *Hedda Gabler* who aims to make himself the foremost authority on domestic industries of Brabant during the Middle Ages, Stavans eschews specialization. His models are polymaths such as Edmund Wilson and George Steiner—foxes rather than hedgehogs, agile thinkers who cannot be reduced to a single line of thought. Susan Sontag, herself an omnivorous intellectual, is said to have quipped that a polymath is someone who is interested in everything, and nothing else. It is invigorating to read Stavans, even as his suppleness—evasiveness?—can be exasperating. To attempt to write about his protean, expanding oeuvre is to be the sorcerer's apprentice besieged by an endless procession of buckets of water.

It would be disingenuous not to disclose that Stavans and I have worked together on a few scholarly projects and that we have known each other for more than two decades. If his grandparents, had, like my grandparents, landed at Ellis Island instead of the port of Veracruz, he would seem to me even more *mon semblable, mon frère* than he already is. But, much as I value Ilan's friendship, this is not an exercise in hagiography. For all his love of Isaac Bashevis Singer's characters, Stavans himself is neither a tzaddik nor a dybbuk. He is more like a prankster. My aim is to study his remarkable career as outsider/insider by surveying his massive, quirky work and examining his recurring themes and his distinctive style.

The Restless Ilan Stavans

ACKNOWLEDGMENTS

My principal gratitude must be extended to Ilan Stavans himself, for the rich material he and his work provide. This is the first book-length study of Stavans, and, while the prospect of writing about a living author can be intimidating, I have to credit him with admirable restraint. Though he never saw a single sentence of the manuscript, he knew of my project but never sought to intrude or influence the book in any way. A faculty development leave from the University of Texas at San Antonio gave me precious time to pursue the necessary research. I want to thank Frederick Luis Aldama, editor of the Latino and Latin American Profiles series at the University of Pittsburgh Press, for his warm encouragement throughout the preparation of the book. I also thank the admirably professional staff at the Press, particularly senior acquisitions editor Josh Shanholtzer, production director Alexander P. Wolfe, and publicist Maria E. Sticco. To my wife, the poet Wendy Barker, my first and wisest reader, any acknowledgment is insufficient.

The Restless Ilan Stavans

1 THE PRODIGY

The opening pages of *A Most Imperfect Union* (2014), Ilan Stavans's graphic contrarian history of the United States, focus on immigration—"a vital part of the American fabric" (7)—and the author's own experience as a twenty-four-year-old immigrant from Mexico. Stavans exploits the opportunity for self-promotion with a cartoon panel depicting three of his own books—*The Hispanic Condition, The Norton Anthology of Latino Literature*, and *El Iluminado*. A sign advertises: "The Ten Thousand Books of Ilan Stavans," and another sign explains: "New titles added hourly" (8).

It is one of many metafictional moments scattered throughout the volume that interrupt the historical narrative to comment on the narrative itself. It is also a refreshing bit of self-mockery, one that pokes fun at Stavans's own image as the Balzac of contemporary American critics, a dynamo of maniacal productivity whom Carolyn See called "a powerhouse of energy," and Reynolds Smith, the executive editor at Duke University Press, described as "more ambitious than 10 men and a mule" (Richardson). In an essay on his experience reading Jewish literature, Stavans identifies himself as a writer of books and then drolly adds: "(perhaps I write *too many* books")" (*Singer's Typewriter* 160). In addition, for a reviewing prank, his Borgesian account of a nonexistent novel by Philip Roth, *The Plagiarist*, he appended a byline that caricatures himself with the claim: "He was described as using performance-enhancing drugs to keep up a frantic, absurd pace of writing. Stavans adamantly denied these allegations before a Congressional committee. His latest book is My Life as an Insomniac (Hyperactive Press, 2008)" ("Philip Roth's New Novel"). Stavans's own father teases him by exclaiming: "What you don't write about, Professor Prolifico!" (*Return to Centro* 25).

Stavans is the author of more than forty books and the editor or translator of more than sixty others, in English and Spanish. In addition to his own titles, Stavans has contributed introductions to dozens of books by other authors, including: Jorge Amado, Homero Aridjis, Mariano Azuela, Jimmy Santiago Baca, Nina Barragán, Alvar Núñez Cabeza de Vaca, Calvert Casey, Cesar Chavez, Martin A. Cohen, Julio Cortázar, Euclides da Cunha, Paquito D'Rivera, John Gregory Dunne, Ricardo Feierstein, Alicia Freilich, Ernesto Galarza, Alberto Gerchunoff, Isaac Goldemberg, H. M. Hudson, Efraín Huerta, Sor Juana Inés de la Cruz, Esther Kreitman, Peter Matthiessen, Octavio Paz, Teresa Porzecanski, Mauricio Rosencof, Domingo F. Sarmiento, Moacyr Scliar, Ana María Shúa, Jacobo Timerman, and César Vallejo. Nevertheless, portraying himself as a disciple of Flaubert and *le mot juste*, Stavans declares without irony: "I'm allergic to verbal excess" (*Disappearance* xi). He has been treating the allergy homeopathically, with a profusion of words.

As far back as 1995, very early in his verbal spree, Stavans began *Bandido*, his study of Chicano activist Oscar "Zeta" Acosta, with the prophetic words: "Excess. Nothing works like excess" (1). If, as William Blake proclaimed, "The road of excess leads to the palace of wisdom," Stavans has, along with Stephen King and Joyce Carol Oates, paved his own path to enlightenment. He has also aroused suspicion, envy, and resentment. As John Updike observed about Oates, "The writers we tend to universally admire, like Beckett, or Kafka, or T. S. Eliot, are not very prolific" (Johnson 216).

Certainly, Samuel Johnson, whom Stavans—calling him "one of the most verbally sensitive, intellectually lucid minds ever to walk this earth" (*Knowledge and Censorship* 76)—reveres above all other lexicographers, might have been wary of such fecundity. "Sir," observed Dr. Johnson to James Boswell, "I never desire to converse with a man who has written more than he has read" (Boswell 41). Stavans's voracity as a reader does exceed his fecundity as a writer—"Being a passionate reader is more liberating, and thus more rewarding, than being a passionate writer," he declares (*Knowledge and Censorship* 112). Nevertheless, he would not have escaped censure by Ben Jonson. "I remember the Players have often mentioned it as an honour to Shakespeare," Jonson recalled, "that in his writing, (whatsoever he penn'd), hee never blotted out line. My answer hath beene, Would he had blotted a thousand" (Jonson 583). Stavans names Gustave Flaubert, who had the luxury to linger for days over a single sentence, as one of his favorite writers, but the blottable errors, calques, and other infelicities scattered throughout thousands of Stavans's pages testify to Balzacian industry more than Flaubertian finesse.

For Gary Saul Morson, a prominent Slavicist at Northwestern University, the man's astounding feracity is largely verbosity: "As Cervantes inserts tedious tales," he says of Stavans's book on *Don Quixote*, "Stavans seems to be filling as many pages as possible" (13). The translator Eliot Weinberger denounced Stavans's short book on Octavio Paz as "unbelievably sloppy" (120). Raphael Folsom, a specialist in Latin American history, arrives at a similar assessment while reviewing two Stavans works, *Art and Anger* and *Imagining Columbus.* "Stavans is an intelligent and learned writer, but not a very careful one," Folsom writes, "and the many errors of fact and style found in these books combined with Stavans's rash judgments and careless analyses to distract the reader from their merits" (361). Furthermore, Bryan Cheyette, a professor at the University of Reading, faults his edition of the *Oxford Book of Jewish Stories* for "critical sloppiness" and "editorial sloppiness" and berates the publisher, Oxford University Press, for having "forgotten the first principles of scholarly rigour."

At twenty-four, Stavans, who was born in 1961, vowed that if he had not published "a major book" by age thirty-three, he would shoot himself (*On Borrowed Words* 6). He repeated that anecdote in Spanish, recounting that "alguna vez me dije que si al cumplir los treinta y tres años no había escrito algo de valor, debía usar la pistol que mi padre guardaba en una caja fuerte" (Stavans and Zurita 46). Though not major in comparison to its successors, his first book in English, *Imagining Columbus: The Literary Voyage,* a study of representations of the Genoese mariner, appeared just in time, in 1993, for its author to bite the bullet. Except for 2013, no subsequent year has lacked a new volume with the byline Ilan Stavans. Into his fifties, he continues to project the aura of enfant terrible, a prodigious generator of youthful energy and ideas who is extravagantly manic even in recreation. He reports that he watched all 64 games leading up to the 2014 World Cup. "It was an exuberant and exhilarating endeavor. An average of one hour and 45 minutes for each meant I was hooked to the TV screen for 112 hours, or 4.66 days" ("Languages of the World Cup").

Acknowledging that he suffers from terrible fear in the face of death and the unanswered questions—"Suffro de un terrible temor hacia la muerte y ante las preguntas incontestadas" (*Prontuario* 138–39)—Stavans declares that he writes in order to be immortalized not in a pantheon but a library: "Si escribo, es porque no quiero terminar en un pantéon sino en una biblioteca" (*Prontuario* 139). He conceives of writing as defiance of mortality. I write, he writes, in order to challenge death, in order to know that time does not pass in vain: "I write in order to prove to myself that I'm not dead, that I'm still here, that every minute I have is mine and that I need to use it in the best possible way in order for the game not to be finished" (*Thirteen Ways* 70). Elsewhere, he writes, in Spanish, that he writes in order to confront death, in order to assure himself that time does not pass in vain: "Yo escribo para enfrentarme a la muerte, para saber que el tiempo no pasa en vano" (Stavans and Zurita 67).

Though he conceives of writing as an attempt to defy death, he also sees it as courting death. "Authors are born with a limited number of sentences to use in a lifetime," he contends. "Once the amount allowed is exhausted, death settles in" (Sokol 194). Writers remain ignorant of the quota each has been assigned, but Stavans has already exceeded the allotment for most other writers—easily more than Emily

Brontë, Georg Büchner, Thomas Chatterton, Raymond Radiguet, and Arthur Rimbaud combined. In Balzac's 1831 novel *La Peau de chagrin* (*The Wild Ass's Skin*), a young man chances upon a magical piece of shagreen that possesses the power to grant any wish. However, each wish that is granted causes the shagreen to shrink, along with the life of the young man. Similarly, Stavans concludes his performance piece *The Oven* (2018) with a mathematical parable about how life is a matter of ergonomics, of deciding when to take the finite actions that are allotted to each of us: "We are all born with a number in our forehead. The number is the total amount of words we have been allocated. Every time we use one, we lose it too. Death is the arrival of zero" (25). With each new sentence that Stavans produces, he thumbs his nose at mortality.

He has frequently described how the loneliness of his first months in the United States was exacerbated by his primitive command of English. Ignorance of the local language meant condemnation to solitude. While wandering the streets of New York, Stavans dared not speak to strangers lest his halting language betray him as a fool. Believing that "el tamaño de nuestro mundo es el tamaño de nuestro vocabulario" (Stavans and Zurita 78), that the breadth of our world is the breadth of our vocabulary, he—already an accomplished writer in Spanish—must have been frustrated by the meagerness of his lexicon in English. It meant that his universe had contracted into the size of a pocket language primer. However, like Joseph Conrad, Aleksander Hemon, Ha Jin, and others, Stavans set himself to mastering the language. Eventually, he was able to anchor his career and his life in English. And, as if to compensate for the reticence of the new immigrant, he became a Niagara of surging words.

The man who admits, "I disliked books when I was a child" (*Art and Anger* 31), developed markedly different passions as an adult. In his study of Acosta, Stavans locates a moment at which the discovery of writing provided purpose to the self-dubbed Brown Buffalo's shiftless life; and the Cartesian motto he ascribes to Acosta could just as well apply to him: "*Escribo, luego existo*" (*Bandido* 48). He exists by and through writing. Stavans marvels at Pablo Neruda, who left behind six thousand pages of poetry, as "impossibly hyperkinetic" (Preface xiv) and, editing a huge selection of the Chilean's poems, puts himself in awe of the "astonishing output" (Neruda xxxix). Elsewhere, he discusses "the astonishingly prolific Argentine César Aira" (*Critic's Journey* 135). In his biography of Gabriel García Márquez, he characterizes the Colombian author as "astoundingly prolific" (*Gabriel García Márquez* 7). His verdict on the productivity of Octavio Paz, who published some 150 titles, is: "simply stunning" (*Octavio Paz* 71).

Stavans's own prolific output is astonishing, astounding, and stunning. It is easy to understand his fascination with Sor Juana Inés de la Cruz, who dazzled her contemporaries in seventeenth-century New Spain with the brilliance of her numerous writings in several genres. But he begins the extensive Introduction he wrote for the Penguin edition of Sor Juana's selected works with a discussion of her famous palinode, *La Respuesta a Sor Filotea* (*Response to the Most Illustrious Poetess Sor Filotea de la Cruz*). Sor Juana, who had succeeded in overcoming the obstacles to a literary woman in a repressive, patriarchal society, was only forty-three when she composed her letter of renunciation. Though she had already produced a substantial oeuvre, she now dedicated her few remaining months to obedience and silence. Stavans is particularly attuned to how, in complying with her religious superior's demand that she cease writing, "she was signing her own death sentence" (Introduction to *Poems, Protest* xi). He himself was thirty-six and not yet ready for silence, not even about Sor Juana, about whom he would publish a monograph, *Sor Juana: Or, the Persistence of Pop*, in 2018.

"*Tenet insanabile multos scribendi cacoethes*," wrote Juvenal (Juvenal, *Satire* VII 140); many suffer from the incurable itch to write. Not many, though, are as hopelessly afflicted as Stavans is with *cacoethes scribendi*. "Everyone is mad," he observes, "the real question is what kind of madness each of us suffers" (*Quixote* 37). Stavans's benign madness is a compulsion to fill page after page after page. According to tradition, Thomas Aquinas said: "*Hominem unius libri timeo*"—I fear the man of one book. Aquinas would have had nothing to fear from Stavans, a man of dozens of books.

In *On Borrowed Words*, the autobiography he published at forty, Stavans attributes his verbosity to growing up in what was, except for his brother Darián, a garrulous family. Every gathering was a gab fest. "How exhausting it all was!" he recalls, as if he were a reader confronting the grown-up Stavans's copious bibliography. "How intimidating!" (141). More generally, Stavans suggests that Jews are genetically talky people. "I wondered," he asked himself as a child, "did G-d deliberately endow us Jews with a tendency not to stop shvitzing and schmoozing?" (141). "No" would have been the reply from Bontsha the Silent, the character in the I. L. Peretz story who, amid overwhelming misfortune, says nothing—if he would have replied at all.

The memoir presents Darián, his junior by only eighteen months, as a kind of inverted doppelgänger. Ilan and Darián grew up together sharing the same bedroom and attending the same school. They were, Stavans recalls, "simply inseparable—como uña y carne, as the Spanish popular saying goes, or, in its English counterpart: 'joined at the hip'" (*On Borrowed Words* 133). However, whereas his brother was a musical prodigy who had no taste or talent for literature or languages, Ilan would excel in both. Whereas Darián suffered from a debilitating stutter, Ilan would never be at a loss for words.

Stavans was hailed in the pages of the *Los Angeles Times* as "a polyglot master of many literary trades" (Tobar) and of the *Washington Post* as: "Latin America's liveliest and boldest critic and most innovative cultural enthusiast" (Manrique). However, part of the price of prolificacy is a certain sloppiness. Homer might not have nodded if he had contented himself with a few haiku. But the abundant Stavans books are riddled with moot assertions and outright errata that might be the products of a hasty pace. It is likely not true that, as Stavans says of "The New Colossus" by Emmas Lazarus: "It's probably the most famous poem in the United States" (*Most Imperfect Union* 108). More famous than "Stopping by Woods on a Snowy Evening"? "The Waste Land"? "The Raven"? "Daddy"? "The Star Spangled Banner"? And it is simply wrong to claim, as Stavans does in *Resurrecting Hebrew* (19), that Old English is a Celtic language. Though he refers to "the endless amendments" to the United States Constitution (*Knowledge and Censorship* 41), there are only twenty-seven. His ecstasy over the figure of Don Quixote leads Stavans to point to "a single, shocking fact: in all of the Western canon, no other novelistic character has ever been adjectivized" (*Quixote* 81). What about *Pecksniffian? Gargantuan? Snopesian? Holmesian? Pickwickian? Pollyannish?*

In two books (*Latino USA* 40 and *Hispanic Condition* 141), he repeats the legend made famous by a *corrido* that Abraham Lincoln's daughter asked the governor of Texas to pardon the Chicano outlaw Gregorio Cortez—without acknowledging that in reality the Great Emancipator had four sons but no daughter. More embarrassing is an error that shows up at a crucial point in *Golemito*, an illustrated children's version of the Jewish Golem legend with a Latino twist. Two boys in Mexico City construct a champion to avenge themselves against bullies. What gives the creature its potency is the Hebrew word for truth, *emet*—אמת—inscribed on its forehead. We are told that the Hebrew word is spelled out "aleph, mem, and tet" (*Golemito* 14). However, the final letter of *emet* is not, in fact, *tet* (ט), but rather *taf* (ת). The truth (אמת) is inadvertently muddled as אמט.

Stavans reveres *Don Quixote*, which he considers one of only two masterpieces in Spanish (*Gabriel García Márquez* 2). (The other is *One Hundred Years of Solitude*, about which he tweeted on February 22, 2017: "It's easier for me to imagine the world without the colour yellow than without this novel"). His enthusiasm for *Don Quixote* leads him to devote an entire volume to the novel as well as to write at length about Domingo F. Sarmiento's *Facundo* as "el Quijote de América" (Introduction to *Facundo* viii), an idealist's vision of how civilization jousted with barbarism in the Argentine pampa. It also sometimes propels him into making hyperbolic assertions. Exulting in the twenty different translations into English of Cervantes's novel, Stavans proclaims, inaccurately: "In fact, other than the Bible, no book has been translated into Shakespeare's tongue as often" (*Quixote* 176–77). Yet the *Divine Comedy* has more than ninety-five English translations, the *Odyssey* seventy. As Stavans reminds us: "Cervantes was not a meticulous craftsman" (*Quixote* 11). And perhaps his passionate contemporary champion ought not to be held to a higher standard.

The Stavans oeuvre has come into the world through some of the most influential publishing houses, including Basic Books, Duke University Press, Farrar, Straus & Giroux, HarperCollins, Houghton Mifflin, Library of America, New Directions, W. W. Norton, Oxford University Press, Penguin, Routledge, Schocken, University of California Press, University of Texas Press, University of Pittsburgh Press, and Yale University Press. In 2010, a particularly productive year, Stavans brought out nine new books, whereas the median number of books *read* by an American in a year is only four ("Mean and Median"). The Stavans engine, which has manufactured several best sellers, is fueled by its own success. Unlike more obscure authors whose book proposals pile up on the desks of jaded assistant editors, he is often solicited by publishers eager to suggest a project and offer a contract. In the case of *The United States of Mestizo* (2013), NewSouth Books was even willing to package a brief essay as a forty-eight-page, stand-alone volume. That same year, the same publisher brought out Stavans's thirty-two-page illustrated children's book, *Golemito*.

Stavans's topics—including lotteries, music, Sephardi culture, travel, the Hebrew language, Cesar Chavez, machismo, Maimonides, dictionaries, food, eroticism, narcocorridos, the Kabbalah, selfies, detective fiction, Jewish gauchos, libraries, evil, Spanglish, picture books, immigration, and God—are dazzlingly diverse. A connoisseur of the subtleties of soccer, he moves deftly from a paean to Portuguese forward Cristiano Ronaldo's performance in the 2018 World Cup to canny analysis of Telemundo announcer Andrés Cantor's use of the future tense. In praise of Cantor, he observes: "His lexicon is immense, his mental reactions are quick, his capacity to describe human behavior is as good as Homer's, his delivery of 22 last names always feels natural, and he inserts all sorts of pertinent anecdotes, historical as well as personal and linguistic, that help enliven the game" ("Sublime Goal").

Stavans's wide-ranging intellectual curiosity, combined with chutzpah, led to the creation of *The Ilan Stavans Library of Latino Civilization*, a series of essay collections he has edited for Greenwood Press "devoted to exploring all the facets of Hispanic civilization in the United States, with its ramifications in the Americas, the Caribbean Basin, and the Iberian Peninsula" (*Latina Writers* vii). The eleven volumes that have so far appeared in the series cover: *Béisbol*; *Border Culture*; *César Chávez*; *Fútbol*; *Health Care*; *Immigration*; *Latina Writers*; *Mexican-American Cuisine*; *Quinceañera*; *Spanglish*; and *Telenovelas*. In ambition, Stavans seems surpassed only by George Eliot's Mr. Casaubon, who, though, never completed his *Key to All Mythologies*. In a conversation with Stavans, historian Iván Jakšić, echoing Isaiah Berlin's famous zoological categories (borrowed from Archilochus, who observed that a fox knows many things, but a hedgehog one important thing), declared: "I am the hedgehog, and you are the fox" (Stavans and Jakšić 121).

With vulpine agility, Stavans has been prominent in a wide variety of roles—

critic, scholar, essayist, editor, publisher, translator, lexicographer, biographer, memoirist, fiction writer, TV host, performance artist, cultural impresario, and teacher. He is also an active blogger and tweeter whose communiqués trigger both adulation and calumniation. Following his account of teaching Shakespeare to inmates at a Massachusetts jail, one reader commented: "This is a beautiful piece, and a refreshing reminder that the Humanities are not abstract or alien to the lives of students." But another reader complained: "What a pompous, elitist, uninformed piece of garble" ("'Gangsta' Shakespeare"). Stavans is a very public intellectual in a way that belies his explanation for why he did not become an actor like his father: "I would rather live in the shadow than in the spotlight" (*One-Handed Pianist* 93). He inhabits bright shadows.

Stavans is personally courteous, amiable, and deferential, though in interviews, lectures, and even his own TV show, he basks in the spotlight. Born Ilan Stavchansky, he adopted Stavans, the stage name of his father, Abraham Stavchansky, as his own. And though he has not followed his father into a career as star of Mexican soap operas, he does regard teaching as improvisational performance. From 2001 to 2006, he hosted a TV program, *La Plaza: Conversations with Ilan Stavans*. Produced by WGBH-TV in Boston and syndicated by other PBS stations, it placed him in front of the camera beside such prominent Latina/o and Latin American luminaries as Isabel Allende, Rubén Blades, Junot Díaz, Ariel Dorfman, Oscar Hijuelos, Elena Poniatowska, Jorge Ramos, and Piri Thomas. In 2015, New England Public Radio began broadcasting a series of interviews called *In Contrast with Ilan Stavans* that has included guests such as lexicographer Peter Sokolowski, political pundit Bill Kristol, illustrator Barry Moser, poet Wendy Barker, novelist Junot Díaz, physician-poet Rafael Campo, biographer William Taubman, journalist Masha Gessen, foreign correspondent Robin Wright, and novelist Min Jin Lee. The spunky intellectual entrepreneur even exploited his passion for *Don Quixote* to lead Dreaming in La Mancha, a group tour of Spain organized by a travel outfit called Scholarly Sojourns.

A current event, such as the anniversary of Cervantes's death or of the bombing of the Jewish community center in Buenos Aires, often inspires newspapers, magazines, radio, and TV to seek Stavans out for a comment. In January 2014, when Argentine Jewish poet Juan Gelman died, the *New York Times* turned to Stavans for a fitting obituary quotation: "He is a gigantic voice in the constellation of Latin American poetry of the 20th century" (Weber). When Pablo Neruda's body was exhumed to determine whether he was murdered by the Pinochet junta, Stavans wrote a piece for the *Times* that is both an elegy for the poet and a denunciation of Latin American tyranny. Bothered by the bombast that passes for contemporary public rhetoric and has made ours "una época del énfasis," he published a column in the *Times* in Spanish that not only complains about the overuse of exclamation points but calls for elimination of the redundant inverted punctuation mark that introduces exclamations in Spanish ("¿Son necesarios los dos signos de exclamación?"). ¡Ay, caramba! In another *Times* column published in that language, Stavans demands more rational orthography and, *de hecho* (in fact), calls for the elimination of the silent "h" in Spanish ("Adiós a la 'h'"). Would readers of José Maria Heredia, Oscar Hijuelos, and Vicente Huidobro consider this an impoverishment of their *herencia*? In 2017, he began writing a weekly column for the *Daily Hampshire Gazette*, a newspaper with a circulation of 16,000 that was founded in 1786. His topics have included terrorism, teaching, aging, Israel, and Catalonia. He is also frequently invited to give public lectures in the United States and abroad.

Moreover, in 2015, in the tradition of monologists such as Eric Bogosian and Spalding Gray and in conscious flirtation with his father's profession as actor, Stavans even transformed himself into the unlikely author and star of a one-man show called *The Oven* that he concocted in collaboration with director Mathew Glassman and other members of the Massachusetts theater troupe Double Edge. Before publishing it with the University of Massachusetts Press, Stavans performed *The Oven* on stages throughout New England and at the University of Oxford and the University of Chicago. In the piece, he recounts how, visiting Bogotá, he is invited by a shaman of the Putumayo tribe to undergo a mystical experience. He is driven for many hours to a remote rural setting, where, ingesting the psychotropic substance ayahuasca, he finds himself metamorphosed into a jaguar.

Despite his cynicism about organized politics, Stavans has increasingly spoken out on public issues. Early in his career, in 1992, he tried to adopt an apolitical stance, writing: "Después de todo, soy un escritor, un esteta y no un polemista" (*Prontuario* 93)—After all, I am a writer, an aesthete and not a polemicist. However, his mature commentaries usually do not isolate the literary from the political. The point of departure for his academic career is a chapter titled "Punto de Partida" (Point of Departure) in his dissertation for Columbia University. And that point of departure in his doctoral study of the detective novel in Mexico is October 2, 1968, when the military massacre of hundreds of students and other civilians in Plaza de las Tres Culturas in Tlatelolco, Mexico City, precipitated a revolution throughout Mexican society.

In 2001, Stavans published an open letter to President George W. Bush pleading for the life of Gerardo Valdéz Mota, a Mexican national who, convicted of murder, awaited his fate on death row in Oklahoma. Instead of trying to make a case against capital punishment, which he recognizes that Bush will not cease to support, Stavans argues that Valdéz Mota was not informed of his right to obtain legal counsel from the Mexican consulate and was therefore denied equal justice under law guaranteed to all defendants regardless of nationality. Valdéz Mota had been convicted of killing a man who made a sexual advance toward him; in an impulsive homophobic reaction, he had in effect othered his victim. Accusing the criminal justice system of othering Valdéz Mota, demonizing him as an alien, Stavans—who must have been particularly moved by the mistreatment of a fellow Mexican—calls for empathy, a faculty nurtured by experience in other cultures. "To the best of my knowledge," he chides Bush, "you have never lived abroad for a sustained period of time. This fact disturbs me deeply. Your travels to foreign countries, even as a tourist, have been very few" (". . . and justice for all" 359). For Stavans, multilingualism and extraterritoriality make one—even and especially the president of the United States—a mensch.

A later president, Donald Trump, who announced his campaign for the White House on June 16, 2015, with an attack on Mexican immigrants as "rapists," has, not surprisingly, aroused Stavans's ire. In an op-ed piece in the *New York Times*, he denounced Trump's disdain for Latinos and his attempts to disparage and suppress the use of Spanish, noting that, unlike his predecessors, the forty-fifth president of the United States is "nefariously monolingual" ("Trump, the Wall and the Spanish Language"). He notes that one of Trump's first acts as president was to expunge Spanish from the White House website. Elsewhere, he has bemoaned the fact that "the nation is commanded by a Latin America-styled tyrant who not only doesn't read (the book he wrote was concocted by someone else) but whose lexicon seems to consist of 750 words" ("Friday Takeaway: Teaching"). He stressed the importance of independent publishing as resistance to Trump, whom he reviled as "the most anti-literary US president in history, in addition to being among the most racist, sexist, and xenophobic" ("Against Narrowness").

Yet, despite his unequivocal opposition to the Trump presidency, it is notable that, for a seminar he taught at Amherst during the fall 2017 semester, Stavans characteristically framed the subject in dialogic terms. Titled "Trump Point/Counterpoint," the project is presented as conversation rather than indoctrination. By his own description:

> This course looks at the Trump Administration from a variety of interdisciplinary perspectives—political science, race and ethnicity, gun rights, culture and the media, religious affiliation, global and local labor trends, gender and reproductive rights, internationalism and foreign relations, linguistics and the arts—offering a forum whereby to ponder, in civil fashion, the clashing liberal and conservative viewpoints that define the United States and the world today. The framework will rotate around the legacy of the Enlightenment as well as theories of individualism, free enterprise, First Amendment rights, American exceptionalism, and neoliberalism, among others. In conjunction with the course, a series of prominent national speakers of both sides of the ideological divide will be brought to campus to share their views in lectures and colloquia to enrolled students and the larger College community." ("Trump Point/Counterpoint")

The Restless Ilan Stavans

For "Globalism and Its Discontents: Point/Counterpoint," a seminar he offered at Amherst in fall 2018, Stavans took a similarly dialectical approach. Though he is himself a fervent champion of cosmopolitanism, an émigré appalled by nativism, his course description promises to take "a balanced view of the debate, using the Socratic method to explore its pros and cons without prejudice" ("Globalism").

Seeing in Cesar Chavez a fulcrum by which to leverage "a more elastic understanding of the Civil Rights Era" (*Cesar Chavez* 12), Stavans has edited a volume of the Chicano leader's speeches and compiled and annotated a collection of Chavez photos. At a time when Latinos were supplanting African Americans as the nation's largest minority group, he was concerned that Americans of Mexican, Puerto Rican, Cuban, Dominican, Salvadoran, and other Latin American backgrounds were still excluded from the national conversation. The lingering effects of slavery and Jim Crow and the election of a black president, Barack Obama, would, understandably, perpetuate a binary view of American identity, but Stavans, as an immigrant from Mexico and a champion of Latino literature, was intent on applying dyes to the duo-chromatic portrait. "The United States has long perceived itself through a black-and-white prism" (*Cesar Chavez* 11), he contends. His mission is to introduce some complicating colors. Seizing on Chavez as a parallel to Martin Luther King Jr., he attempts to remind his readers not only that Delano deserves to be remembered along with Selma, that El Movimiento was perhaps as significant as the struggle for racial equality, but, more generally, that Latinos must not be erased from American history or excluded from American culture. So he appropriates Chavez, the most influential of Chicano figures, as his paragon, "a model in the larger fight against poverty and corporate abuse" (*Cesar Chavez* 12). Though he concedes that Chavez was "human in his defects" (15), he never specifies any of those defects except for Chavez's opposition to immigration. Earlier, in *The Hispanic Condition*, Stavans had antagonized many admirers of the farmworkers' leader by describing him as "a good Hispanic dictator, intolerant, undemocratic authoritarian" (81). However, unlike several studies that examine the complexities of Chavez, Stavans's hagiographic *Cesar Chavez* ignores his hero's authoritarianism and inconsistencies that sometimes undermined the struggle of the Chicano farmworkers he was leading.

Stavans is the narrator of his own recorded books—*The Novel That Invented Modernity* (2014) and *God: A History* (2014). Nevertheless, though a talented soliloquist, he enjoys staging conversations, in print and in person. "You're famous as a *conversador*," exclaims one of his interlocutors, Frederick Luis Aldama (Stavans and Aldama, ¡Muy Pop! 88). Stavans even invented a fictive coauthor, Zuri Balkoff, for his novella *Talia y el cielo* (1989). "I am a passionate lover of the dialogue as a revealing form of intellectual engagement" (Stavans and Gracia 2), he explains. Despite the deft use of dialogue by Plato, Denis Diderot, David Hume, and other Gentile writers, Stavans claims that there is something distinctively Jewish about the form. He notes how Argentine novelist Ana María Shua's *The Book of Memories* "pays tribute to a recognizable device in Jewish letters—more specifically, in Yiddish literature: the unfolding of the story while two guys talk" (Stavans, Introduction to *Book of Memories* xi). As examples, he mentions Mendele Mokher Sforim's *Fishke the Lame*, Sholem Aleichem's *Tevye the Dairyman*, Chaim Grade's "My Quarrel with Hersh Rasseyner," and Isaac Bashevis Singer's "The Cafeteria." He notes: "This device opens all sorts of possibilities: Jewish life is approached as a debate, a clash of opinions, an encounter" (xi–xii).

An expression of delight in exchanging and contesting ideas, Stavans's own use of dialogue is both Socratic and Midrashic. He explains his attraction to the form by noting the discoveries it engenders: "What I love about a dialogue is the interaction it fosters, the encounter of two minds who, through words—words in the present and words that hopefully will last—discover something new about themselves and the other. The encounter provokes all sorts of reactions. Those reactions are serendipitous: they are the result of accident and cannot be replicated. Internal and outside circumstances come together in this mano a mano encounter. And they trigger fresh, spontaneous ideas" (Stavans and Gracia 3). Even when offering a seminar at Amherst on a monolingual, xenophobic president he obviously opposes, Stavans conceives of it in dialogic terms, titling it "Trump Point/Counterpoint" and conceiving it as collective examination, not exhortation. In contrast to Trump, the autocrat who fires and maligns dissenters, he praises Cesar Chavez as "a true duelist" (Foreword to *Sal Si Puedes* xxxviii).

In a zestful double metaphor, Stavans likens a book-length conversation in Spanish that he begins with Juan Villoro to a jazz duo and to pairing off a roomful of socks of varied colors: "Me gustaría que estas conversaciones fueran como el jazz: espontáneas, como si los dos estuviéramos ambos en un cuarto oscuro repleto de calcetines en el cual nuestro objetivo es buscar pares del mismo color" (*El oja en la nuca* 3). Driven by a dialogic imagination, he has been unusually collaborative, sharing the bylines of his books with Verónica Albin, Lalo Alcarez, Frederick L. Aldama, Harold Augenbraum, Marcelo Brodsky, Mordecai Drache, Joshua Ellison, Jorge J. E. Gracia, Iván Jaksic, Adál Maldonado, Steve Sheinkin, Neal Sokol, Juan Villoro, Roberto Weil, Xiao Hai, Miguel-Angel Zapata, and Raúl Zurita. He is remarkably generous in exchanging ideas and inspiring others. Though they seem conversational and even desultory, his book-length dialogues are usually carefully contrived and edited written exchanges. It is unlikely, for example, that, during the course of a meandering chat with Verónica Albin, Stavans would have come up with this precisely phrased bit of erudition: "Dr. Johnson in his *Dictionary of the English Language* of 1755 calls attention to the Latin root for 'dictionary,' *dictionarium*, then states: 'A book containing the words of any language in alphabetical order, with explanations of their meaning'" (*Knowledge and Censorship* 56) or that he would be able, off the top of his head, to recall that "the OED defines the word *kiss* thus: 'To press or touch with the lips (at the same time compressing and then separating them), in token of affection, or greeting or as an act of reverence'" (*Love & Language* 48).

Stavans is so taken with the possibilities of dialogue that he concludes *Dictionary Days* with an imaginary conversation that he stages with the "Great Cham of Eighteenth-Century Literature," Samuel Johnson. In addition, near the climax of the psychotropic experience he recounts in *The Oven*, he beholds two theologians, Rabbi Eliezer and Rabbi Yehoshua, who appear to him to be twins and take opposing sides on fundamental philosophical issues. According to Rabbi Eliezer: "The universe is full. No matter what humans do to it, it will always be full. It depends on us to find its fullness." Responding to a vision of the universe as broken vessels, which, contrary to the teachings of Kabbalah, can never be repaired, Rabbi Yehoshua offers the opposing view: "No, the universe is broken. It has always been broken. We can't fix it even if we want to" (*The Oven* 27). The back and forth between the two is yet another example of how Stavans gropes his way toward truth through dialectic.

However, when he is not able to organize or fantasize dialogues with others, he is conversing with himself. He published *Talia y el cielo* in Mexico under the twin bylines of Ilan Stavans and a fictive collaborator, Zuri Balkoff. He had earlier signed the pseudonym Zuri Balkoff to radical leftist pieces he wrote for the Mexican newspaper *La Jornada*, at the same time that he was publishing less clamorous, more measured pieces in other newspapers under the byline Ilan Stavans. It was a kind of personal psychomachia that Stavans was conducting by projecting himself onto two contrasting personalities.

In his ambitious novella *Talia in Heaven* (whose English translation is included in *The One-Handed Pianist and Other Stories*), a Canadian Jew named Talia Kahn journeys to a country called Paranagua, where she becomes involved with two men who seem to be halves of a split personality. One, a professor of medieval and Renaissance philosophy at the Universidad Autónoma de Paranagua, is named Ilan Stabans, while the other is a Marxist revolutionary named Igal Balkoff. Stabans, who embraces an "introspective, pacific, humanist and blessed ideal" (*One-Handed Pianist* 108) is at odds with Balkoff, who dedicates himself to militant collective action for social justice. When Stabans invites Talia to the movies, it is, appropriately, to see Robert Louis Stevenson's *Dr. Jekyll and Mr. Hyde*, the 1920 adaptation directed by Victor Fleming and starring Spencer Tracy and Ingrid Bergman. However, that 1920 movie was, in fact, directed by John S. Robertson and Nita Naldi, whereas it is the 1941 version that was directed by Fleming and featured Tracy and Bergman. In any case, the Jekyll/Hyde references underline the dialogism that is central to this fiction and to Stavans's career in general. "In order to make the fictional account tangible, the two sides of my self needed to have a role as authors" (Sokol 17), he explained. The Stavans oeuvre is a continuing conversation not only between

Stavans and others, but between Stavans and other versions of himself, including Zuri Balkoff. He explains: "I have always had the feeling of living somebody else's life" (*One-Handed Pianist* 191), and much of his writing is an interior dialogue with his imaginary doppelgänger. Two selves—Mexico and the United States; Jewish and Latino; Spanish and English; outsider and insider—collide, converse, and concur.

Reading a Stavans book often creates the sensation of eavesdropping on *Conversations with Myself*. Detractors might substitute Norman Mailer's title *Advertisements for Myself*. But it is remarkable how frequently the pronoun "I" appears in Stavans's prose, how often he incorporates himself into his discussions. He has not been shy about including his own work in collections of Latin American fiction, Latin American essays, and Jewish stories that he has edited. And he has stepped forth as the most visible—and maligned—champion of the validity of Spanglish, dubbed by Holly R. Cashman as "Spanglish's ambassador to the Spanish-speaking world, its faithful defender and its successful agent" (219).Pairing his own keyboard with that of a Nobel laureate, he immodestly titled a collection of essays on Jewish culture *Singer's Typewriter and Mine* (2012). And, tracing the history of the United States, in *A Most Imperfect Union*, he audaciously and flippantly inserted himself into key moments of its development. A generally positive review of Stavans's book *The Hispanic Condition* contends: "This book manages to be worthwhile despite the obtrusive ego of the author" (Stevens-Arroyo). Reviewing *On Borrowed Words*, Carolyn See points out: "It might be that instead of 'autobiography,' this memoir concerns the yearning of a man who has yearned for much of his life—in four languages—just to be the center of attention."

Though Stavans might seem to have little in common with the raffish Chicano rebel Oscar "Zeta" Acosta, he was drawn to write about his life precisely because of the opportunity to examine himself through the lens of an inverted doppelgänger. "He was the embodiment of what I've tried repeatedly to leave out of my life: the cult of the body, life as a bohemian trip through altered states of consciousness," Stavans explains. "His tics are an open encyclopedia of sixties Chicanismo. What I detest in him is obviously what I'm most afraid of in myself: excess in politics, excess of self-pity, excess of self-glory" (Heller). He coyly named a key character in *Talia in Heaven* "Ilan Stabans." And he even made himself the principal character in a graphic murder mystery, *El Iluminado* (2012), a detective caper that is set in Santa Fe, New Mexico, and playfully characterizes itself as "*The Da Vinci Code,* with matzo and salsa picante" (Stavans and Sheinkin 39). While trying to tie an unsolved death to the history of New Mexico's crypto-Jews, he is chided by a rival professor for having "already done enough damage with Spanglish and your comics and the rest, mister polymath" (Stavans and Sheinkin 170).

It seemed inevitable that Stavans would devote a book to the excessive phenomenon of selfies, the fad for photographic autoportraits facilitated by the ubiquity of cell phones, and title it *I Love My Selfie* (2017). He includes several of his own selfies, including an unflattering image of him recumbent, his paunch exposed. Obsessed and repelled by the self, Stavans subjects it to unrelenting scrutiny. In another book, Stavans recounts a recurring nightmare throughout his life in which he is tormented by mirrors. "To this day, I don't like looking at myself in photographs because I always find something bizarre about myself" (Stavans and Gracia 9–10), he confesses. Through dozens of books, many of them dialogues that serve as intellectual mirrors, Stavans tries to subdue the terror of his self-regarding gaze. All of his writing is speculative, a journey through the looking glass, a confrontation with the dreadfully revealing speculum.

2 THE STAVANS PARADOX

More than three decades after moving to the United States, Stavans still speaks of himself as a foreigner, a cherished state of mind that not even naturalization can expunge. "I am, I will always be, a Mexican in the United States," he proclaims. "An alien—the Other" (*Hispanic Condition* 198). Vaunting the pleasures and values of travel, he prides himself on not being at home anywhere. "Being an outsider," he insists, "is an integral part of me" (Stavans and Fonseca). Even tenured and domiciled in western Massachusetts, he travels widely and frequently.

In *Reclaiming Travel* (2015), written with Joshua Ellison, Stavans reflects on the tonic disorientation that comes with wanderlust. Respecting the critic's duty to be forever on the move, he is a foe of stasis, a proverbial wandering Jew. It is appropriate that the name he gave the independent publishing house he founded in 2013 is Restless Books. Specializing in translations, the company advertises that its mission is to "deliver stories of discovery, adventure, dislocation, and transformation" that reflect "the restlessness of our multiform lives" (Restless Books). Proudly global in its ambitions, the publishing operation is not an endorsement of "America First."

On November 11, 2016, three days after the election of a president whose ignorance of and indifference to the world beyond American borders he finds repugnant, Stavans blogged a reaffirmation of his guiding principles as publisher: "Now more than ever, the mission of Restless Books is clear: to expand our understanding of a world that seems narrower, to amplify voices that are suppressed or neglected, and to fight the trend toward isolating ourselves through publishing superb literature from around the globe. Our focus is not on publishing books with a specific message, but rather finding stories that express our trying times, that make us see things anew, that surprise and move us, that speak to our restlessness" ("Now More Than Ever"). The challenging poetry, fiction, and nonfiction from Chinese, French, German, Hebrew, Hungarian, Icelandic, Persian, Polish, Russian, Spanish, Uzbek, and other languages that Stavans and his colleagues at Restless Books make available to Anglophones reject reading as a restful activity. In *Reclaiming Travel*, the book that Stavans coauthored with Ellison, the publishing house's cofounder, the two declare: "Our belief is that we urgently need to reclaim a definition of restlessness—'stirring, constantly, desirous of action'—that signifies our curiosity toward the world, our eagerness to explore outside the safe confines of the familiar (Stavans and Ellison 6). In 2017, Stavans created Yonder, an imprint within the press that specializes in bringing the same restless experience to younger readers by making available works for children and adolescents that were written in languages other than English. Since the company is based in a renovated can factory in the Gowanus section of Brooklyn, where five full-time employees share space with another adventurous independent publisher, Archipelago Books, Stavans's active role as publisher requires his own restless movement back and forth between his home in western Massachusetts and the firm's office in southern New York.

He presents himself as the scourge of comfort and its corollary, complacency. "My most patent fear," he proclaims fearlessly, "is—has always been—that of becoming too comfortable anywhere. Literature is born out of discomfort. After all, comfort is the mother of complacency" (Stavans and Fonesca). Yet even Stavans sometimes backslides into languorous longings, as when he declares that "the truth is that what I like most is my comfort: the comfort of home that grants me proximity to my family, my book, my desk" (*Knowledge and Censorship* 11). And, unlike many other academic celebrities who seem to change their addresses almost as often as their underwear, Stavans has stayed at Amherst—albeit with many excursions far afield—for more than three decades.

But gadflies cultivate discomfort, in themselves and others. A professor who is the scourge of the professoriate and writes wistfully about the adversarial culture of the *Partisan Review* intellectuals, he begins his 2014 graphic survey *A Most Imperfect Union*—subtitled *A Contrarian History of the United States*—by admitting: "I have frequently been described as a contrarian—an adjective that pleases me, to be frank, for I enjoy looking beyond embellishments and fabrications to the truth (or at least what I think is the truth at the heart of things)" (xi). Though he became a citizen of the United States in 1994, Stavans styles himself a staunch foe of borders and flags: "I don't believe in the superstition we call nationalism," he declares (Stavans and Jakšić 125). Not entirely at home in the United States, Mexico, or anywhere else, he declares, "I like being foreign" (*Borges* x). Being foreign is, for Stavans, not a matter of passport but a state of mind, as well as a vocational responsibility.

Multilingualism liberates Stavans from the confinements of any one language, just as travel makes him geographically extraterritorial. A strategy of willful alienation, of keeping himself foreign, emancipates him and widens his perception. In a conversation with his friend Davin, an Irish patriot, James Joyce's Stephen Dedalus expresses an impatience that Stavans would likely share: "You talk to me of nationality, language, religion. I shall try to fly by those nets" (Joyce 182). Nevertheless, throughout his writings, Stavans, repeatedly betraying his universalist aspirations, paints himself into discrete boxes—Hispanic, Jew, Hispanic Jew, academic, American—only to apply turpentine to the edges and effect his escape.

In his Introduction to *The Schocken Book of Modern Sephardic Literature* (2005), Stavans faults Abraham Joshua Heschel for a simplistic dialectic in which everything is defined by its antithesis and "the Sephardim are everything that the Ashkenazim are not" (xvi). It is tempting to resort to binary oppositions when trying to characterize broad phenomena such as entire cultures, though perhaps the original sin is the very effort to characterize broad phenomena at all. Frequently, and especially in *The Hispanic Condition* (2005) and *What Is la Hispanidad?* (2011), Stavans himself makes grand pronouncements about the Hispanic mentality, and, by conceptualizing it as the antithesis of Anglo culture, he sometimes falls back on the "Manichaean paradigm" (xvi) that he faults Heschel for. His own account of Jewish culture is binary—Ashkenazi/Sephardi, with little recognition of Mizrahi, Ethiopian, Indian, Kaifeng, and Romaniote Jews. But then he attempts to dissolve his neatly contrived polarities.

Because Richard Nixon had been such a staunch foe of accommodating the Communist regime in Beijing, his visit to China found wider support than it would have if the thirty-seventh president had not based his career on red-baiting. Similarly, by establishing his career as a leading commentator on Hispanic and Jewish themes, Stavans can count on wide attention to his gesture of renouncing group identity. The Stavans Paradox is that his very success as a professional Hispanic and Jew created a platform from which, in the name of a liberating universalism, he can attempt to deny—or at least obfuscate—the categories of Hispanic and Jew. Soon after calling Cesar Chavez "the most important Hispanic American political figure of the twentieth century" (Foreword to *Sal Si Puedes* xxxviii), he admires his ability to transcend ethnic niches: "His Mexicanness, he showed us—and now I see—is a lesson in universality" (lii). By editing the *Oxford Book of Jewish Stories*, Stavans attempted to establish a particularist canon, though it is not entirely clear just what his criteria are for determining a "Jewish story." Perhaps the Jew is simply synecdoche for the human being, and the parochial inevitably becomes the global. But, according to Bryan Cheyette, his selection is "arbitrary and ill-defined," and the collection ends up as a celebration of "a spurious universality."

The Hispanic Condition (1995), which was lumped by David G. Gutierrez with other "rather superficial compendia of current trends in Hispanic art and literature" (Gutierrez 101) and described by Peter S. Temes as "an argument for accepting social identity broadly, in the most cosmopolitan terms," is too superficial to be entirely satisfying to Hispanists but not broad enough to be genuinely cosmopolitan.

Writing from Barcelona, Leonardo Valencia Assogna described Stavans's effort as journalistic rather than analytic, written in nervous, agile prose appropriate as a general introduction for readers not already familiar with the subject: "Está escrito con una prosa nerviosa, ágil, afincada más en la exposición de trazo amplio del periodismo cultural que en la serenidad del ensayo analítico. Es un libro plagado de anécdotas y referencias bien descritas para el neófito en el mundo—o los mundos— de la injerencia que tienen en Estados Unidos los inmigrantes de países latinoamericanos" (Assogna 211). In the series of essays that constitute *The Hispanic Condition* Stavans expatiates on colonialism, machismo, *West Side Story*, homosexuality, bilingual education, immigration, and other topics. He offers perceptive commentary on such figures as Gregorio Cortez, Oscar Hijuelos, Eugenio María de Hostos, Richard Rodríguez, and José Antonio Villareal. He surveys the histories and traditions that distinguish Tejanos from Californios from Cubanos from Boricuas from Dominicanos from Salvadoreños and others. But then he tries to collapse them all into one convenient category: Hispanic.

For many years, Stavans, a linguistic determinist, preferred *Hispanic*, which defines the group by its relationship to Spanish, over *Latino*, a term preferred by political activists and that he complained connotes a faint, unimportant connection to Roman culture. Nevertheless, he uses *Latino* in the titles of *Growing Up Latino* (1993), *Latino USA* (2000), *Encyclopedia Latina* (2005), and the *Norton Anthology of Latino Literature* (2011). In *The Hispanic Condition*, he offers a distinction not widely embraced: Latinos live in the United States, Hispanics in the rest of the world. He asks: "Life in the hyphen—what do we, as Latinos, want from the United States, and what do Anglos expect from us?" (170). Elsewhere, he often uses *Hispanic* and *Latino* interchangeably, though by 2018, in *Latinos in the United States*, he was now declaring: "I prefer the term 'Latino'" and stating that he would reserve the term "Hispanic" for "people living in the Hispanic world" (xxvii). It is unlikely that a Caraqueño, a Madrileña, a Chilango, and a Porteña would all think of themselves as "Hispanics."

Stavans's impossible—Quixotic!—objective is to pin down the quiddity of *la hispanidad* (*la latinidad*?)—Hispanicity. To do so, even while acknowledging the diversity that the term encompasses, he tosses people of a wide variety of races, classes, and cultures together under the amorphous rubric *Hispanic*. To speak of "the Hispanic condition" or *la hispanidad* is to adopt an essentialist position, to assume— fallaciously: (1) that there are qualities shared by all Hispanics, and (2) that those qualities are unique to Hispanics. Though Stavans describes his project as "a set of reflections on our plural culture" (*Hispanic Condition* 2), he easily loses sight of its pluralism. Being Hispanic is a matter of contingencies, not essences.

His essentialist position becomes clear when, in *What Is La Hispanidad?* he describes the *telenovela* as "an enormous machine that promotes the concept of la hispanidad in a subliminal fashion. Think of it as an endless quantity of kitsch with a message." Asked by his interlocutor: "What kind of message?" Stavans replies: "That Hispanic civilization is about overwrought emotions. Also, that loyalty and hypocrisy are the essential feelings defining it" (Stavans and Jakšić 110). A civilization is a complex of overlapping and evolving elements. It is a mistake to ascribe necessary and sufficient conditions to it.

Cuban American philosopher Jorge J. E. Gracia throws Stavans's essentialist position into stark relief during their book-long dialogue in *Thirteen Ways of Looking at Latino Art* (2014). Stavans and Gracia bounce ideas off each other as they contemplate, successively, thirteen works by Latino artists. Using the occasion to pontificate again on *la hispanidad*, Stavans concedes: "Hispanics might come in different shapes." But, he insists, "They share an essence. That essence, in my view, tends toward the melodramatic and is frequently derivative" (33). His interlocutor takes a nominalist stand against universals and cautions against generalizing about entire cultures. In his own book *Latinos in America* (2008), Gracia follows Jean-Paul Sartre in asserting individual existential freedom: "There is no such a thing as a Latino, or even a Mexican identity, for there is no essence to them. There are only individual identities forged by individual humans" (11).

In his dialogue with Stavans that constitutes *Thirteen Ways of Looking at Latino Art*, Gracia offers an empirical argument against Stavans's attempt to erect cultural labels into discrete universal categories. "I do not think that one can find any trait that is common to all phenomena that are classified as Hispanic," Gracia contends. "The reason is that what we call Hispanic civilization is not something that has an essence, that is a set of properties that are common to all things called Hispanic" (Stavans and Gracia 32). Similarly, one cannot find any trait that is unique only to phenomena that are classified as Hispanic. Stavans and Gracia remain at loggerheads over universals, and, as the chapter ends, they agree to disagree. However, if Gracia is right, it is foolish to expound on "Latino art"—or to present oneself as an authority on Jewishness and *la hispanidad*. According to Gracia, neither has a substantive reality.

By the time he came to write *Latinos in the United States: What Everyone Needs to Know*, Stavans's position on ethnic identity had hardened. The very format of the book, published in 2018, is a betrayal of the dialectical method on which he prides himself. Its very title presupposes that the sage author is dispensing incontrovertible truth. *Latinos in the United States* consists of a series of questions and answers in which the questions constitute not genuine interrogation as much as merely pretexts for providing information. "When did 'Hispanic' emerge?" "What is Latinidad?" and "Which states have the largest Latino concentration?" Stavans asks himself and proceeds to furnish the answers. It is catechism more than Talmud. Moreover, as Richard Feinberg complains, "Too often its language is imprecise and its facts incorrect. (The Mexican businessman Carlos Slim is rich, but not the richest person in the world, at least not anymore. The Cuban dictator Fulgencio Batista did not lose an election in 1952; he canceled it)" (200).

A triangle has an essence. All triangles—equilateral, isosceles, or scalene—are polygons with exactly three angles, and only triangles are polygons with exactly three angles. A centaur has an essence. All centaurs are creatures with the upper body of a human and the lower body of a horse, and only centaurs possess that peculiar structure. However, unlike triangles and centaurs, human communities are motley clusters of individuals with overlapping characteristics. They are more like Venn diagrams than Platonic Forms. Acknowledging the heterogeneity of the Hispanic community, Stavans declares: " Diversity is our flag: We are blacks, Spaniards, Indians, mulattos, and mestizos" (*Hispanic Condition* 32). Nevertheless, the folly of Stavans's basic enterprise, to isolate "the Hispanic condition," is evident in his bizarre claim that "unlike the African and Asian minorities in the United States, we [Hispanics] share one language (Brazilians, French Caribbeans, and Guayanans excepted); one cultural background; and a single religion, Catholicism" (*Hispanic Condition* 32). Speaking scores of indigenous and European languages, Hispanics do not share one language, not even Spanish or English. Many speak Nahuatl, Zapotec, Quechua, and other non-Indo European tongues. Only in the most nebulous notion of "culture" can people whose origins are in Mexico, Guatemala, Peru, Cuba, El Salvador, Argentina, Puerto Rico, Colombia, and the Dominican Republic be said to share "one cultural background."

But the most obvious flaw in the assertion of a Hispanic essence comes in Stavans's statement that *we* share a "single religion, Catholicism." Stavans, who has based a significant part of his career on being Jewish, is certainly not Roman Catholic. And, though he goes on to acknowledge that "other faiths coexist in the Hispanic world and lately a number of believers have switched to Protestantism" (*Hispanic Condition* 32–33), that verbal legerdemain does not succeed in obscuring the falsehood of the claim that Hispanics "share a single religion." In another book, describing Mexico's syncretism of European Christianity with indigenous beliefs, Stavans again identifies himself with the dominant religion, stating that "our Catholicism revolves around the Trinity but with an Indian emphasis" (*Return to Centro* 3). Though the outsider author might try to appropriate the first-person-plural pronoun to present himself as an insider, to make the interloper "I" a "we" speaking for the entire community, he himself is living, Jewish proof that the claim for a single, shared faith is untrue.

In the Epilogue to *Latinos in the United States*, Stavans lists one hundred artifacts that collectively, he contends, embody Latino experience. Despite his personal campaign throughout his career to recognize a Jewish presence within the cultures of Latin America, not a single one of the artifacts on his list is Jewish. He does, however, include a crucifix, a retablo with Catholic iconography, a Virgin del Cobre figurine, a torture instrument used by the Holy Office of the Inquisition, and a potion from a santería ritual. Stavans even lists a Spanish translation of the Qur'an as one of the one hundred objects essential to an understanding of Latinidad. However, the one item on the list with any vague Jewish connection is Leonard Bernstein's score to *West Side Story*. Though Stavans wrote the Introduction to Martin A. Cohen's groundbreaking study *The Martyr: Luis de Carvajal, A Secret Jew in Sixteenth-Century Mexico* and devoted his own entire book, *El Iluminado* (Stavans and Sheinkin) to recounting the martyrdom in New Spain of the crypto-Jew Luis de Carvajal the Younger, and translated into English Carvajal's memoir, that memoir is missing from the list. So, too, are other artifacts of Jewish Latino culture such as: a menu from El Nosh, the fusion food truck that has popped up in Miami and New York; an inauguration photo of Eric Garcetti, the Mexican American Jew who served as mayor of Los Angeles; and a copy of "The New Colossus," the famous poem written by Emma Lazarus, a Sephardic Jew. Stavans might even have included his own *On Borrowed Words*.

He sometimes uses "we" in a kind of Whitmanesque attempt to be the spokesman for all Americans, Hispanics and non-Hispanics. "We Americans are cutthroat egoists looking to advance our own person agendas" (*Most Imperfect Union* xiii), he declares, though a reader might wonder whether every single American is indeed a cutthroat egoist, whether other nationalities also include cutthroat egoists, and whether Stavans as individual really is one. Use of the first-person plural is particularly notable throughout his discussion of "the Hispanic condition." Many of his oracular pronouncements are moot, if they are not vaporous. When he states, for example, "We are Quixotic, anarchic, and fatalistic at heart, imprisoned in our own individuality and sense of time, eternal inhabitants in a traumatic garden of history" (*Hispanic Condition* 94), he does not tarry for empirical proof. Surely there is at least one Hispanic whose heart beats to the rhythms of Sancho Panza more than Don Quixote, who is anal more than anarchic, and who, like Tomás Rivera, is open enough to the future to write: "Con miedo, yo creo que uno es capaz de todo" (I suppose if you're scared enough, you're capable of doing anything) (Rivera 58, 132). If it means anything, being "imprisoned in our own individuality and sense of time, eternal inhabitants in a traumatic garden of history" is a universal condition, rather than anything uniquely Hispanic. And though he asserts that "our psyche is carnivalesque, introspective" (*Hispanic Condition* 199), the Bavarian culture that produced both Oktoberfest and Thomas Mann and the Slavic culture that produced both Maslenitsa and Fyodor Dostoevsky are surely as carnivalesque and introspective as the Hispanic.

So, although Stavans has much of value to say about particular personalities and phenomena, his project of isolating a cultural chromosome unique to Hispanics and shared by all Hispanics is problematic in two ways: It makes ontological assumptions unsupported by evidence, and it proffers its idiosyncratic author as a representative figure. Much of what Stavans has to say about Hispanics in general consists of nonnullifiable hypotheses. How does one go about testing the contention—like the Freudian tenet that patricide and sex with one's mother are the repressed desires of all males—that "Courting women with serenades and flowers, laying them in bed, undressing them, fucking them—no better term applies: *cojer, chingar, mancillar*—only to throw them out the door, that's every Hispanic male's hidden dream" (*Hispanic Condition* 109)? *Every* Hispanic male? No Japanese or Nigerian males? Since Stavans employs "we" throughout his discussion, is that a personal confession? It hardly comports with the complexities of desire he discusses in *Love & Language* (2007) or with his description in that book of the powerful, exclusive love he feels for his wife Alison. How does one go about testing the claim that "linear and circuitous, inextricable and impenetrable, the maze—complex, curved, distorted, wandering, winding, with constant double tracks—is a map of the Latino psyche" (*Hispanic Condition* 93)? Perhaps the best support for the claim is that Stavans's own sentences and arguments are labyrinthine, cryptic, and elusive.

Presuming to speak for "the Hispanic condition," a Jewish immigrant from Mexico writes himself into insider status. But Stavans also prizes the liberating perspective of the foreigner, as if only the traveler can experience the world without constricting borders. For all the trouble he takes to construct and populate his conceptual categories (Hispanic, Anglo, Jew, Sephardi), he is most enthusiastic about tossing them together, in a triumph of *mestizaje.*

3 STAVANS THE HISPANIC

Who in the world am I?
Ah, *that's* the great puzzle!
—*Alice's Adventures in Wonderland*
(Carroll 18)

The character named Professor Contreras, who delivers a snark attack on Stavans in *El Iluminado*, mocking him as "mister polymath," could stand for the author's numerous adversaries within academe. They are abundant and influential enough for the *New York Times*, in an article subtitled "'The Czar of Latino Literature and Culture' Finds Himself under Attack" (Richardson), to have reported on the resentment felt by many tenure-track specialists in Latina/o Studies toward an interloper on their scholarly turf. The grandson of Jewish immigrants from Ukraine and Russia who was born and raised in Mexico City, Stavans grew up in Colonia Copilco, a middle-class neighborhood that he characterizes as "a secure, self-imposed Jewish ghetto, an autistic island where gentiles hardly existed and Hebraic symbols prevailed" (*Hispanic Condition* 195). Elsewhere, he describes the childhood home in which he was raised—"in a bubble, unconscious of the Gentile environment around me" (*On Borrowed Words* 84)—as "a secure, self-imposed Jewish ghetto (a treasure island) where gentiles hardly existed. . . . We lived in an oasis completely uninvolved with things Mexican" (*One-Handed Pianist* 182). Though he struggled as an undergraduate at the Universidad Autónoma Metropolitana to find solidarity with fellow Mexicans, "I must confess," he confesses, "never to have learned to love Mexico" (*One-Handed Pianist* 186).

In describing "the kind of Mexican upbringing I received: Europeanized, cosmopolitan, universal" (*Return to Centro* 17), Stavans opens himself to the hostility of Hispanic advocates who recoil at universalism as a denial of the specificity of *la hispanidad*. Though sometimes attacked for not being anchored enough in Hispanic culture, he prefers to situate himself within a more capacious global culture, explaining: "Our global culture is not about exclusion and isolation but about cosmopolitanism, which etymologically derives from the Greek terms cosmos and po-lis, a planetary city" (*Latino USA* xi). What Stavans finds particularly appealing about the figure of Octavio Paz is his "deep-seated cosmopolitanism" (Introduction to *Monkey Grammarian*). Addressing Carlos Fuentes in an early essay about him, he credits the Mexican novelist, who lived for extended periods in Chile, France, Pana-ma, Switzerland, and the United States, for teaching him that it is not necessary to live in Mexico in order to be Mexican: "Al fin y al cabo, de ti y de nadie mas aprendi que para ser mexicano hoy es innecessario vivir en Mexico" (*Prontuario* 97). Stavans would later conclude that it is not necessary to live anywhere in particular in order to be a critical thinker. He rejects the parochialism of national and ethnic cheerlead-ers; Mexican novelists must not be restricted to writing only about conquistadors, banditos, and drug runners: "Just as Shakespeare set his plays in England as well as in Italy, Denmark, Greece, France, and other places," he argues, "the scope of the Mexican writer ought to be the entire world" (Introduction to *Monkey Grammarian*).

Devoid of any strong feelings about his native land, Stavans announces that "the Mexican soil is meaningless to me—utterly inconsequential" (*On Borrowed Words* 34). He was an outsider in Mexico, where he found himself defined as a Jew, though he was never a very pious one. Neighborhood kids teased him for his fair hair and Eastern European background, calling him *el güerito* and *el ruso*. Palestinian sympa-thizers threw tomatoes at him. In the United States, to which he emigrated in 1985, at age twenty-four, Stavans was a Mexican, though, pale-skinned and alien to the barrios of East LA and San Antonio, he lacked Chicano street cred. Moreover, he was suddenly and for the first time consigned to the category "Hispanic." During his childhood and adolescence, "The fact that I was Mexican mattered less than the fact that I was *un judío*. Conversely, the moment I arrived in New York my Jewishness ceased to matter and, ironic as it might be in New York, I suddenly became a *mex-icano*—a Mexican among other Hispanics: Colombians, Argentines, Dominicans, and Puerto Ricans" (Sokol 100). Almost twenty years after his emigration, Maria Eugenia Sevilla, writing in the Saltillo publication *Palabra*, was still referring to him as "el filólogo mexicano."

A white Latino, Stavans has used his background in and distance from both Mex-ican and Jewish cultures to serve as an interpreter of each and as a bridge between the two. In *El Iluminado* (Stavans and Sheinkin), he recounts the less propitious fate of another Jew in Mexico, the martyrdom of Luis de Carvajal the Younger. He re-casts it as a graphic mystery story in which a character named Ilan Stavans is a somewhat bumbling detective tracking down the truth about a centuries-old hidden Diaspora within Latin America. A crypto-Jew, Carvajal left old Spain with his fam-ily for the relative freedom of New Spain (i.e., Mexico). However, when he came out as a Jew, Carvajal—along with his mother, siblings, and others—was burned at the stake by the Inquisition in an elaborate auto-da-fé in Mexico City's Zocalo in 1596.

In the tradition of Borges's fictions about nonexistent books and of his own literary prank, a review (first published in the Purim edition of the *Forward*, March 4, 2009, and later collected in *Singer's Typewriter and Mine*) of *The Plagiarist*, a nonexistent novel by Philip Roth, Stavans considered creating a review of an imaginary dual biography of Luis de Carvajal the Younger and his uncle, Luis de Carvajal the Older, a formidable conquistador who became governor of Nuevo Leon. However, as he explains in the Introduction he wrote to Martin A. Cohen's *The Martyr: Luis de Carvajal* (2001), he first checked to see whether such a biography existed. That is how he learned about Cohen's solidly researched book, from which he drew information and inspiration for *El Iluminado*, a graphic novel that portrays the residual effects of colonial persecution of Jews. Stavans also took on Latin American anti-Semitism in another graphic novel, *Golemito*. Set in Mexico City, it is the story of how Sammy Nurko is taught by his friend Ilan to construct a golem to protect him against neighborhood bullies who prey on Jews. Stavans might have drawn inspiration from his own adolescent experience in Mexico City in the paramilitary Jewish defense group called Bitakhon. In 2018, long after his expatriation, Mexico City elected its first Jewish mayor, Claudia Sheinbaum Pardo.

His own youthful acquaintance with Alejandro García Durán de Lara, a charismatic and enigmatic cleric nicknamed Padre Chinchachoma (Man without Hair), was the inspiration for another graphic novel, *Angelitos*. As a young Jew eager to repair injustices in a society to which he felt he did not fully belong, Stavans volunteered to help the scruffy Catholic priest minister to the homeless children of Mexico City. Created in collaboration with artist Santiago Cohen, *Angelitos* is set in 1985, against the backdrop of an earthquake that devastated the area. An earnest college student loosely based on Stavans himself becomes involved with Padre Chincha's legally ambiguous work among the city's street urchins.

Reviewing Jacobo Timerman's memoir *Prisoner without a Name, Cell without a Number*, Stavans presents the author, an outspoken Jewish journalist imprisoned by the Argentine junta in 1977, as another Jew trying to negotiate a space within a Latin American culture intolerant of his ethnic background. The persecution of Timerman intensified his Jewishness; he was, according to Stavans, "an assimilated Jew whose victimizers turned him into a symbol of survival that is, to a degree, the voice of the approximately 1,500 Jewish desaparecidos in Argentina" (*Singer's Typewriter* 137). Similarly, Mauricio Rosencof, who was finally released in 1985 after spending thirteen years in prison in Uruguay, is for Stavans yet another victim of Latin American anti-Semitism (*Singer's Typewriter* 157–59). Moreover, the eighty-five people killed on July 18, 1994, in the bombing of AMIA, the Associación Mutuel Israelita Argentina in Buenos Aires, whom Stavans memorializes in his fotonovela *Once@9:53am*, represent a failure to forge a bond between *la judeidad* and *la latinidad*. Identifying with the victims, Stavans recalls: "I remember thinking to myself, was this bomb meant to kill me?" (*Once@9:53am*). He, too, was a Jew in a Latin America rife with anti-Semitism, though he has lived to write about it, and, in writing about it, overcome the chasm separating Jew and Latino. It is understandable that he seeks consolation in the work of Latin American Judeophiles such as Homer Aridjis, Jorge Luis Borges, and Mario Vargas Llosa.

Stavans, though, is a successful link not only between Jewish and Latino worlds, but, more generally, between North and South, Anglo and Latino. By editing *Mutual Impressions: Writers from the Americas Reading One Another* (1999), a gathering of essays by writers below the Rio Grande on writers from the North and of *norteamericanos* on writers from the South, he has presented himself as a literary Pan American Highway, a mediator between two halves of a fractured hemisphere. In the collection, John Updike comments on Augusto Roa Bastos, Grace Paley on Clarice Lispector, Robert Bly on Pablo Neruda, and Thomas Pynchon on Gabriel García Márquez, while José Marti weighs in on Walt Whitman, Jorge Luis Borges on Nathaniel Hawthorne, Mario Vargas Llosa on Ernest Hemingway, and Carlos Fuentes on William Styron. The editor of the prestigious *Norton Anthology of Latino Literature*, Stavans has also positioned himself as what a correspondent in the Spanish newspaper *El País* called "el zar de la cultura Latina" (Carbajo). If *The Hispanic Condition* (1995) established him as an authority on its titular subject, the 2018 publication of *Latinos in the United States: What Everyone Needs to Know*—by the prestigious Oxford University Press—confirmed and consolidated his position. In the latter book, he is much less tentative, more definitive, in the questions about Latino experience that he poses to himself and confidently answers. The text is a monologue in the form of a dialogue, an auto-catechism in which Stavans himself provides both call and response to such provocative questions as: "Should Latinos be understood as a byproduct of colonialism?" "What happened at the Alamo?" "What were the Zoot Suit Riots about?" "How should the concept of Aztlán be understood?" "Why deport undocumented immigrants to Mexico if half of them come from other countries?" "Is there a Latino literary tradition?" The self-assured, unequivocal answers to each that Stavans provides could certainly be challenged. For example, his claim that "Latinos are not only the fastest-growing group in America; they are also the biggest" (*Latinos in the United States* xxv) is, according to U.S. Census figures, only half right; Asians are in fact the fastest-growing group in the United States.

However, to some, Stavans remained an upstart *mexicano* who lacked sufficient authority to claim the mantle—conferred on him by *The Chronicle of Higher Education*—of "the Skip Gates of Latino studies" (Heller). Like Henry Louis Gates Jr., the maestro of African American studies at Harvard who revived *Transition* as a lively journal of the African diaspora, Stavans, based at another elite Massachusetts institution, Amherst College, founded *Hopscotch: A Cultural Review* as a literate forum with a Latino base. Published by Duke University Press, *Hopscotch* advertised itself as "an invitation to look at past and present Hispanic cultures anew, to revisit its multifaceted history and identity by reencountering its diverse roots and heritage—from indigenous peoples to European settlers, from African slaves brought during colonial times to the subsequent waves of immigration from Asia, the Middle East, and Western and Eastern Europe. The journal covers art, literature, cinema, and politics and begins to consider the many faces of Hispanics in the world today" (*Hopscotch*).

In the very first issue of *Hopscotch*, published in 1999, Stavans announces: "Our goal is to explore in depth, and with total honesty and a sense of social responsibility, the complexities of our Hispanic heritage, emphasizing what we share with others as well as what makes us unique" ("Convocation" 2). That issue offers many of the topics that Stavans would pursue throughout his career—Alberto Gerchunoff, multilingualism, José Vasconcelos, Octavio Paz, Spanglish. And just as Gates was general editor of the hugely successful *Norton Anthology of African American Literature*, Stavans was commissioned to define another crucial canon by editing the *Norton Anthology of Latino Literature*. Gates himself contributed a generous blurb to *The Essential Ilan Stavans*, praising him as "an old-fashioned intellectual, a brilliant interpreter of his triple heritage—Jewish, Mexican, and American." However, symptomatic of the academic establishment's discomfort with Stavans, when *PMLA*, the official publication of the Modern Language Association that rarely publishes reviews, took the unusual step of publishing a review of his *Norton Anthology*, it was not positive. Titled "What Was Latino Literature?" and written by Kirsten Silva Gruesz, a professor at the University of California Santa Cruz, the review-essay compared Stavans's project unfavorably with Gates's *Norton Anthology*, contending that "the Latino *Norton* is hobbled by the lack of any prior powerful literary-historical narrative with which to contend. Canonicity happens here without a clear sense of its relation to periodicity" (Gruesz 336). In another influential academic journal, *Latino Studies*, Stavans was berated for naively equating culture with language and with perpetuating a colonialist mentality toward the peoples of the Western Hemisphere (Sáez).

Professors who labor for years on a single monograph to be read by dozens of other specialists might have envied the broad popular success of a cultural parvenu who often writes on deadline and by invitation. Unlike Stavans, few of them were represented by a literary agent. Unlike Stavans, who founded Quixote Productions in 2003, few of them were CEO and chairman of their own production company. Unlike Stavans, who founded Restless Books in 2013, few academics ran their own publishing house. Like Andrew Carnegie, Steve Jobs, and Oprah Winfrey, he is an outsider whose entrepreneurial ingenuity and pluck pushed him inside a charmed circle. Publication of *The Essential Ilan Stavans* by Routledge in 2000, only ten years after graduate school, when he had written or edited "only" fifteen books, seemed to some premature canonization. Stavans is a popularizer, an eager practitioner of what the French call *haute vulgarisation*. Convinced that writing for nonspecialists is a lowly calling, many members of the academy dismiss *haute vulgarisation* as an oxymoron. When Eliot Weinberger called Stavans "a professional explainer of Mexico for gringos" (124), he did not intend it as a compliment.

But more germane is the question of appropriation. "He doesn't come from within the culture," noted Tey Diana Rebolledo, a professor of Spanish at the University of New Mexico. "He's not Chicano. He's a Mexican. He hasn't been in the movement since it started, so he's a little bit of an outsider" (Richardson). That movement is *El Movimiento*, the Mexican American struggle for civil rights that had mostly run its course by the time Stavans moved to New York in the 1980s. The Mexican American Legal Defense and Educational Fund, founded in 1968, and La Raza Unida, founded in 1969, had already been leading campaigns for educational opportunity, fair employment practices, and voting rights for almost two decades. Though he wrote at length about two of its leaders, Cesar Chavez and Oscar "Zeta" Acosta, Stavans never participated in the intense organizational meetings, trials, and marches that helped improve economic, educational, and political conditions for Mexican Americans, nor did he suffer personally from those oppressive conditions. It did not enhance his reputation among Chicanos that he criticized Chicano leaders, including Chavez, for their opposition to immigration, which, he argued, "is the equivalent of being against their own origins. And their connection with Mexico, where many of them traced their roots, was faulty, disengaged, and even negligent" (Foreword to *Chicano Movement* ix).

It is notable that, recognizing his own outsider status, Stavans is drawn to the figure of Fred Ross, the gringo activist who found in Chavez, the Chicano farmworker, a perfect complement to his ambitions. Ross founded the Community Service Organization that Chavez would use as his initial base of power. In the Introduction to the collection of Chavez speeches that he edited, Stavans states: "Ross was looking to recruit an insider not only able to speak Spanish but to communicate with Mexican workers on their own terms" (Chavez xiii). He attributes the success of the farmworkers' movement and perhaps of El Movimiento in general to the Ross-Chavez partnership of outsider and insider. "The friendship between the two is an example of an invigorating cross-ethnic encounter" (Chavez xiii).

Though he claims that, like Chavez, they can use it as an "engine of success," Stavans accepts Paz's assessment that Chicanos suffer from an inferiority complex. His blog about the subject drew an angry online response from someone using the handle "pele10" and offering this blunt advice: "Perhaps you should remove yourself from your Ivory Tower and spend some time with some real Chicanos" ("Do All Chicanos Have an Inferiority Complex?"). The cumulative resentment of Latino activists toward interloping commentators is epitomized in the preface to *Harvest of Empire: A History of Latinos in America*, in which author Juan González, a founder of the Puerto Rican Young Lords, vents his exasperation: "At some point, I grew tired of having our story told, often one-sidedly, without the passion or the pain, by experts who had not lived it" (González xvii). For González, experts who had not lived it are not experts at all. They adopt what he calls "the safari approach, geared strictly to an Anglo audience, with the author as guide and interpreter to the natives encountered along the way" (xvii). González must imagine Stavans in pith helmet leading privileged foreigners in encounters with the exotic natives of Latinidad.

According to Louis Mendoza, now a professor at Arizona State University, Stavans is an "opportunist and interloper—an ambitious outsider who has managed to present himself as authentic spokesperson for cultures and experiences he knows only from a distance" (79–80). Mendoza attacks what he calls "Stavans's contempt for his subject and audience" (84). He complains that Stavans's portrait of Acosta is "devoid of scholarly rigor" (79) and that it betrays "a pathological characterization of Chicanos" (85). Stavans explicitly denies any attempt at an objective biography of Acosta, whom, projecting an imaginary intimacy, he prefers to call Zeta. Instead, his book gathers his impressions of a man he never met. "It's better not to have known him," he explains. "Better to imagine who he was, to reinvent him" (*Bandido* 13). His reinvention of Zeta as "redundant, extravagant, and immoderate . . . an immoralist, a hedonist, a ferocious beast trapped in the skin of a Mexican-American" (13) irritated Mendoza and others.

Though Stavans insists: "I'm a lover of Hispanic civilization" (*Quixote* 206), his own characterization of Latin America as "a stumbling civilization fixated on the past, the illegitimate child of Iberian conquistadores, thirsty for gold and power, and Indian mothers raped while the crucifix stood as witness" (Stavans and Augenbraum xi) provides ammunition to his Hispanist detractors. Attempting "to represent Hispanic civilization as a fiesta of types, archetypes, and stereotypes," Stavans explains that he wants to avoid "an official, impartial tone, embracing instead the rhythms of carnival" (*Latino USA* xv). Embracing those rhythms, he rejects the role of dispassionate observer. There is a crucial distinction between the scholar of carnival and its celebrant. When Vladimir Nabokov applied to teach at Harvard, Roman Jacobson quipped to his colleagues: "Gentlemen, even if one allows that he is an important writer, are we next to invite an elephant to be Professor of Zoology?" (Boyd 303). For conscientious scholars, Stavans is the elephant in their classroom.

Part of the tension between Stavans and his critics derives from a dialogic imagination that expresses itself more readily in conversation than proclamation. Stavans resists being pinned down to any immutable thesis. "History, of course is a kaleidoscope where nothing is absolute," he declares, absolutely. "The human past and present are far more malleable than the future" (*Latino USA* xv). If, echoing

Heraclitus, he regards human experience as "neverending flux" (12), he would be foolish to attempt to reify and fossilize it. Born under the sign of the question mark, he prefers questions to answers and indeed conceives of life as interrogative rather than declarative. "La vida es una serie de preguntas sin repuesta" (Stavans and Zurita12), he asserts, though in effect asking: "Is life a series of questions without response?" Stavans's playful, evasive style is both invigorating and exasperating. Those eager to refute him find no unequivocal assertions there to refute. There is an irritating inconstancy to a sprightly writer who declares that "the only principle I uphold is the principle to disagree" (*Love & Language* 231). Is it possible to be both a brilliant gadfly and a frivolous dilettante? When he calls musician Paquito D'Rivera "*un burlón*, a trickster" (Foreword to *My Sax Life* vii), he is also describing himself. *Elenchus*—the Socratic method of posing question after question—is unquestionably valuable for philosophy and pedagogy, though Socrates himself goaded the hegemonists of Athens into terminating him.

The combination of outsider and insider is an ideal for Stavans. He sees it not only in the symbiotic relationship of Fred Ross and Cesar Chavez but also within himself. However, to many of his critics, Stavans is an interloper presuming the privileges of an insider. And central to the discomfort that many academic specialists feel toward Stavans is opposition to cultural appropriation, a conviction that outsiders are not entitled to impersonate or exploit members of a group to which they do not belong. Many Americans of good will would now agree that white entertainers who perform in blackface and sports teams that adopt Native American mascots are abusing their privilege in order to objectify and exploit the Other. Binjamin Wilkomirski's *Bruchstücke: Aus einer Kindheit 1939–1948* (*Fragments: Memories of a Wartime Childhood*) (1995) was widely hailed as an important Holocaust memoir, until it was exposed as a fraud, whose author, in fact named Bruno Grosjean, had tried to pass off the horrific ordeal of a Jewish boy as his own. The case of William Styron is more complex. In 1968, when he published *The Confessions of Nat Turner*, an account of an 1831 slave rebellion in Virginia narrated by its leader, Styron presented it as a novel and made no claims for it as an authentic memoir. However, as a privileged white man, he was fiercely attacked for presuming to write in the voice of an enslaved African. Similarly, Danny Santiago's *Famous All Over Town* (1983) is an award-winning novel that depicts the grittiness of life within the barrio of East LA. It was beginning to be hailed as a classic of Chicano literature, until an article in the *New York Review of Books* unmasked Danny Santiago as Daniel Lewis James, a talented and empathetic Anglo whose experience as a social worker provided him with firsthand knowledge of his subject.

Did Styron's and James's backgrounds as outsiders negate their literary achievements? Formalists maintain that the text stands on its own, independent of the identity of its author. Others insist, instead, that literature is a social construct that cannot be understood apart from how it is implicated in the lives of its authors and readers. Knowing that Saul Bellow wrote *Henderson the Rain King* without ever having visited Africa is as pertinent to our experience of that novel as knowing that Joseph Conrad served as captain of a steamboat in the Belgian Congo is to our reading of *Heart of Darkness*. Nevertheless, there is something odd about the fact that, after gushing that *The Education of Little Tree* was "a loving story about a boy growing up with his grandfather and learning about nature and speaking to the trees. And it's very spiritual," Oprah Winfrey abruptly removed the book from her influential recommended reading list after discovering that its author was not, as claimed, Forrest Carter, but rather Asa Earl Carter, a white supremacist (Italie).

No one gazing at Michelangelo's marble *David* in Florence's Galleria dell'Accademia cavils that, unlike his subject, the sculptor was neither Hebrew nor adept with a slingshot. But when Dana Schutz exhibited *Open Casket*, a painting based on the famous photograph of Emmet Till's battered corpse, at the Whitney Biennial in March 2017, it seemed to many a racial transgression. Protesters gathered outside the Whitney Museum, and Josephine Livingston and Lovia Gyarkye voiced their indignation on the *New Republic* website: "For a white woman to paint Emmett Till's mutilated face communicates not only a tone-deafness toward the history of his murder, but an ignorance of the history of white women's speech in that murder—the way it cancelled out Till's own expression, with lethal effect" (Tomkins 35). Whites got away with killing Emmett Till, but a white artist was forced to apologize for having painted him.

In her keynote address to the Brisbane Writers Festival on September 8, 2016, Lionel Shriver lashed out against the taboo proscribing cultural appropriation. "I am hopeful that the concept of 'cultural appropriation' is a passing fad," Shriver, a self-described German American novelist, declared, "people with different backgrounds rubbing up against each other and exchanging ideas and practices is self-evidently one of the most productive, fascinating aspects of modern urban life" (Shriver). Shriver was immediately and harshly condemned by partisans of identity politics. One, Yassmin Abdel-Magied, did not even wait for Shriver to conclude her talk. Present in Brisbane, she walked out on what she called "a *celebration* of the *unfettered exploitation* of the experiences of others, under the guise of fiction." Abdel-Magied, whose 2016 memoir *Yassmin's Story: Who Do You Think I Am?* describes growing up in Australia as a Muslim migrant from Sudan, dismissed Shriver's talk as "a poisoned package wrapped up in arrogance and delivered with condescension" (Abdel-Magied). In 2018, Shriver continued to affront conventional wisdom by attacking a plan by Penguin Random House to ensure greater diversity among its authors. Fallout this time included the decision by the literary magazine *Myslexia* to drop her as a judge for its short fiction contest.

Trench warfare over cultural turf continued in May 2017, when Hal Niedzviecki was pressured into resigning as editor of *Write*, the magazine of the Writers' Union of Canada, after publishing an editorial that proclaimed: "In my opinion, anyone, anywhere, should be encouraged to imagine other peoples, other cultures, other identities. I'd go so far as to say there should even be an award for doing so—the Appropriation Prize for best book by an author who writes about people who aren't even remotely like her or him" (Leck). Niedzviecki's column, published in an issue of *Write* devoted to First Nations writers, provoked enraged reactions, including this statement by the Writers' Union of Canada: "We are angry and appalled by the publication. . . . In the context of working to recruit writers historically marginalized in the union, this essay contradicts and dismisses the racist systemic barriers faced by Indigenous writers and other racialized writers. This is especially insulting given that this issue features the work of many Indigenous writers" (Dundas).

However, unless writers are free to imagine others' experiences and sensibilities, literature is reduced to narcissism. William Shakespeare's greatness derives in large part from what John Keats called his negative capability, his genius for projecting himself into a vast array of personalities unlike himself—Othello, Juliet, Falstaff, Richard III, Lady Macbeth, Shylock, Cleopatra, Caliban, Cordelia, Nick Bottom, et al. As Stavans has pointed out, Shakespeare pilfered everything. "Is there anything he wrote that was truly original?" he asks, in an essay celebrating the way Justin Bieber pilfers Reggaeton in the pop song "Despacito" ("Friday Takeaway: Ilan Stavans on 'Despacito'"). Honest outsiders—Alexis de Tocqueville on the infant United States, Wendy Doniger on the history of Hinduism, Bernard Lewis on the Middle East—bring a keen eye to phenomena that those immersed in a culture might take for granted.

In response to complaints that when he writes about Acosta, Sandra Cisneros, Cherrie Moraga, or Rolando Hinojosa he is a cultural poacher, Stavans does not deny that he is an outsider. "I'm a Mexican Jew with no direct connection to Chicanos other than my intellectual pursuits," he admits. How dare he, a Latin American but not a Latino, presume to coedit the collections *Growing Up Latino: Memoirs and Stories* (with Augenbraum, 1993) and *Lengua Fresca: Latinos Writing on the Edge* (2006)? Questioning Stavans's authority to offer glib generalizations about a culture he approaches as an interloper, Arturo Madrid, a professor at Trinity University, asks: "Do all émigré Mexican academics have a superiority complex, feel they are experts on Chicanos, and believe they can opine and generalize about us?" ("Do All Chicanos Have an Inferiority Complex?"). Stavans, however, resents a kind of groupthink among professional Chicano scholars by which "any alien poring over their affairs is automatically described as an intruder. There's a certain allergy to free inquiry and enterprise in the community" (Stavans and Jakšić 77). The fact that he was born in Mexico City rather than Laredo or Hialeah should not disqualify him from editing the four-volume *Encyclopedia Latina* (2005) or serving as editor in chief of the Latino Studies section of *Oxford Bibliographies*. The whiteness of William L. Andrews, Keith Byerman, and Werner Sollors has not prevented them from making significant contributions to Black Studies. The leading cetologists are not whales.

Even while distancing himself from others, Stavans often asserts his solidarity with them. Riffing on Oscar "Zeta" Acosta's 1973 novel *The Revolt of the Cockroach People*, he observes that "in the eyes of the American mainstream we are cockroaches" (¡*Muy Pop!* 34). Professor Madrid might be tempted to retort: "What do you mean 'we,' Kemo Sabe?" In a similar presumption of group identity, throughout *The Hispanic Condition*, his 1995 study of the *mentalité* shared by Latinos and Latin Americans throughout the Western Hemisphere, Stavans employs the first-person plural. Even while painting a dismal picture of the Hispanic mind as "a carnival of sex, race, and death" (*Hispanic Condition* 121) and suffering from "a lack of openness, debate, and respect for other people's opinion" (173), he includes himself in the group portrait. "We are Quixotic, anarchic, and fatalistic at heart," he declares about all Hispanics, including himself. His contention that "we suffer from a frightening absence of critical thinking" (180) is proven false by the critical statement itself, but it does testify to the author's conflicting centripetal and centrifugal impulses. He longs to be part of the group as well as its detached interpreter and oppugner.

Stavans is an iconoclast who delights in smashing the idols of his own tribes. Although his academic background is in departments of Spanish, he dismisses almost everything except for *Don Quixote*, of which he is a passionate devotee, written in Spain: "As a tradition, Spanish literature is uninspiring" (Durán 153). Nor does he recommend the writings of Carlos Fuentes, Jose Emilio Pacheco, and Juan Rulfo for the most brilliant depictions of his native country. "The best literature I know about Mexico," he insists, "is by European and U.S. writers: Andre Breton, Jack Kerouac, Graham Greene, Joseph Brodsky, Antonin Artaud, Katherine Anne Porter, Malcolm Lowry, Harriet Doerr" (*Inveterate Dreamer* 257).

Stavans describes the martyred Selena Quintanilla-Pérez, whose adoring fans proclaimed her the Queen of Tejano Music, as "melodramatic, cheesy, overemotional" (*Riddle of Cantínflas* 5). Dubbing Isabel Allende, perhaps the best-selling contemporary Spanish-language novelist, "the queen of melodrama," he dismisses her books as "derivative." Her success he attributes to "a shrewd literary agent in Barcelona, first-rate—and well-paid—translators, and the undefeatable formula: *repeat, repeat, repeat*" (Sokol 90). Frida Kahlo, the Mexican painter whose tormented life and grotesque work posthumously inspired Fridamania, was, according to Stavans, "pure fake" (*Riddle of Cantínflas* 54). So, when he calls Sandra Cisneros "the Frida Kahlo of her generation" (*Hispanic Condition* 73), it is no compliment. He describes Cisneros's most famous book, *The House on Mango Street*, as "a simple, cliché-filled coming-of-age tale by and about Hispanic women, uncomplicated and unapologetic"

(*Riddle of Cantínflas* 115) and disparages it as "slick and sentimental, sterile and undemanding" (84). While enumerating its faults, he does call her later novel *Caramelo* "brave, kaleidoscopic, and ambitious" (*Critic's Journey* 60).

Though Cherrie Moraga is an icon of Chicano activism, Stavans rejects her conception of literature as a weapon and contends that, "not surprisingly, her opinionated work is highly predictable and often stale" (*Art and Anger* 84). He contrasts Moraga with Judith Ortiz Cofer, who, in his unfashionable assessment, "may well be the most important Hispanic writer in English today, the one who will happily leave behind ethnic writing to insert herself and her successors in a truly universal literature, one that is neither apologetic nor falsely 'representative'" (79). The fact that Ortiz Cofer was Puerto Rican, not Chicana, probably did not endear Stavans to his harshest detractors. Similarly, he has accused American Jews of naiveté and complacency. And, though he praised *The Pagan Rabbi* and *The Puttermesser Papers* for possessing "a degree of complexity at odds . . . with all other women writers active in the English language today" ("On Separate Ground" 2), he dismissed Cynthia Ozick, one of their most respected icons, as being "needlessly baroque—a show-off" (Sokol 38).

Thus, even while employing the categories of ethnicity to approach writers, Stavans wants to dismiss them in favor of a transcendent universalism. When accusations of sexual misconduct against Junot Díaz threatened to tarnish all Latino writers, Stavans refused to regard him or anyone else as representative of Latinidad, and he refused to restrict any writer to representing only Latinos. "The purview of any artist is the world," he declared, "not only the small corner that served as a cradle" ("Episode 24"). The fact that Judith Ortiz Cofer cannot be contained within an ethnic category is what appeals to him about her. "She has no national or racial vanity," he contends (*Art and Anger* 79). Though a naturalized citizen of the United States, who, after a sojourn in Israel, rejected aliyah, Stavans resists the label of *norteamericano* as much as *mexicano*. He is in fact a dual citizen of the United States and Mexico. "I've always perceived myself as *anational* . . . not atheistic, but *anational*," he proclaims (*Love & Language* 230).

Nevertheless, for all his cosmopolitanism, Stavans has little to say about writers who are not either Jewish or Latino. Though he states: "Of course, [Of course?] my favorite American book of all time is *Moby-Dick* by Herman Melville" (*Most Imperfect Union* 90), he contents himself with that brief assertion, sans explication. Relatively obscure works such as Mauricio Rosencof's *The Letters That Never Came* and Antonio Muñoz Molina's *Sepharad* receive more sustained attention from Stavans. It would be fascinating to see Stavans grapple with *Sir Gawain and the Green Knight* or *Faust* or *The Iliad*. What might he have to say about echt Latin literature—that is, the poetry of Catullus, Horace, Ovid, and Virgil?

Even the most ambitious universalist cannot be expected to be conversant with all the literature produced throughout the world. And Stavans's silence about *Dream of the Red Chamber, Tale of Genji, Ramayana*, Omar Khayyam, and Léopold Senghor is understandable and pardonable. He approaches cultures from the vantage point of the Americas and Europe. However, Stavans's willful dismissal of French literature is both surprising and deplorable. He does proclaim himself a "passionate devotee" of Michel de Montaigne as "the first, authentic autobiographer" (*I Love My Selfie* 22). He acknowledges his debt to the inventor of the personal literary form he himself loves to employ, the sixteenth-century essayist who "freed us from superstition and explored the limits of rational thinking" (22). However, the rest of the sumptuous body of French literature—Balzac, Baudelaire, Hugo, Molière, Proust, Voltaire, et al.—remains unexplored territory for Stavans. He attempts to explain that cavernous gap in his literary culture by stating that, as a general principle: "I gravitate toward writers connected with larger ideas, whose craft is delivered with linguistic precision. (This makes me somewhat allergic to French literature, for instance)" (Stavans and Newman).

Linguistic precision is not a notable feature of Stavans's beloved *Don Quixote*, which is padded with inconsistencies and longueurs. He has admitted that during his adolescence he found Cervantes's novel "untidy, unfocused, and monotonous" (*Quixote* xv). Furthermore, it is, au contraire, the French who in fact coined the term "le mot juste." Stéphane Mallarmé, whose evocative but elusive poetry begins to disappear once a single word is altered, is legendary for his verbal fastidiousness, as is Gustave Flaubert, who was so obsessive about the right word in the right place that he reworked one scene in *Madame Bovary* fifty-two times. Anyone looking for verbal precision—and concision—(i.e., wit) need look no further than the maxims of the Duc de la Rochefoucauld and the classically restrained tragedies of Jean Racine. Moreover, anyone who, like Stavans, returns again and again to questions of personal identity, essence, and contingency ought to read Jean-Paul Sartre and Albert Camus.

Despite—or because of—such lacunae, Stavans wants to position himself as an anomalous Jew and Latino privileged to comment on Jewish and Latino cultures and serve as an intermediary between the two. At the same time, he presents himself as a cosmopolitan proclaiming his freedom to dissolve such parochial categories. The question that Stavans poses as the key to Octavio Paz's career—"How to be simultaneously an outsider and an insider in the society we happen to be part of?" (*Octavio Paz* 26)—haunts his own chameleon career as well.

4 STAVANS THE JEW

Für mich ist die unverfälschte jüdische Religion
wie alle anderen Religionen eine Incarnation
des primitiven Aberglaubens. Und das jüdische
Volk, zu dem ich gerne gehöre und mit dessen
Mentalität ich tief verwachsen bin, hat für mich
doch keine andersartige Dignität als alle anderen
Völker. Soweit meine Erfahrung reicht ist es
auch um nichts besser als andere menschliche
Gruppen wenn es auch durch Mangel an Macht
gegen die schlimmsten Auswüchse gesichert
ist. Sonst kann ich nichts "Auserwähltes" an ihm
wahrnehmen.

(For me the Jewish religion like all others is an incarnation of the most childish superstitions. And the Jewish
people to whom I gladly belong and with whose mentality I have a deep affinity have no different quality for
me than all other people. As far as my experience goes,
they are no better than other human groups, although
they are protected from the worst cancers by a lack of
power. Otherwise I cannot see anything "chosen" about
them.)

—Albert Einstein, trans. James Randerson

For much of Stavans's early life, Jewishness was something he could take for granted, the way that water is nothing special to a herring. The son of "the first openly Jewish actor on Mexico's professional stage" (*On Borrowed Words* 103), Stavans is the product of a Yiddish-speaking household, a Bundist day school (the Colegio Israelita de México), and the Jewish Theological Seminary. As a teenager, he joined Bitakhon, a paramilitary Jewish group organized for self-defense against anti-Semitic thugs in Mexico City. He remains openly mindful that relatives of his died in the Holocaust and of how, but for the contingencies of history, his direct forebears, too, might have shared the gruesome fate of millions of European Jews in the twentieth century. Much of Stavans's energy has been devoted to editing literature by Jews and writing about it, as well as about both Yiddish and Hebrew. He plays with and does not take entirely seriously the remote possibility that Cervantes was a *converso* and that Jorge Luis Borges might have had Jewish ancestry, but he describes his Amherst seminar on *Don Quixote* as a Talmudic study of the text, sentence by sentence. In 2005, *The Schocken Book of Modern Sephardic Literature* received the National Jewish Book Award, signifying that the book, if not its editor, was Jewish. In 2008, the Jewish newspaper the *Forward* named Stavans, along with such celebrities as Ruth Bader Ginsburg, Adam Sandler, and Jon Stewart, to its list of the fifty most influential Jews. "My Judaism is the key through which I open the different doors I cross" (Durán 150), he has explained.

Stavans has written extensively about the Jewish writers of Latin America, from Alberto Gerchunoff to Isaac Goldemberg and beyond. He has been the North American reader's impresario for Jews who write in Spanish and Portuguese. He has also written at length about European Jews such as Sholem Aleichem, Isaac Babel, Elias Canetti, and Danilo Kiš. However, he has had almost nothing to say about canonical and popular North American writers such as Saul Bellow, E. L. Doctorow, Allen Ginsberg, Joseph Heller, Tony Kushner, Philip Levine, Bernard Malamud, David Mamet, Chaim Potok, and Mordecai Richler. Though he calls Philip Roth "a writer I admire profoundly" (before denouncing him, along with Woody Allen as "kings of parochialism") ("Is American Literature Parochial?), he has—apart from the sophomoric stunt of reviewing an imaginary Roth novel—had almost nothing to say about Roth's formidable oeuvre.

Though he does write at length about other Jewish writers and about Jewish languages, Stavans does not attempt the full frontal explanation of what *la judeidad* means that he does for *la hispanidad*. Usually, when pressed to explain what makes something Jewish, he falls back on a variation of Justice Potter Stewart's definition of obscenity: "I know it when I see it." And, intent on countering Ashkenazi myopia with at least some recognition of Sephardi history, he sees Jewishness in a wide range of persons and phenomena across space and time. American Jewish consciousness, he complains, tends to be limited to the Holocaust and Israel. Yet a reading of Paul Auster, Michael Chabon, Joshua Cohen, Nathan Englander, Jonathan Safran Foer, Nicole Krauss, Gary Shteyngart, and Lara Vapnyar would not support that argument. Nevertheless, surveying recent movies, television, and literature, he complains that American Jews, beneficiaries of this country's pluralism and tolerance, have become increasingly insular in their interests. He insists on emphasizing the true heterogeneity of Jews within a multicultural society. Likening Jewishness to jazz, a flexible, improvisational state of mind, he suggests that Herbie Hancock's description of the musical form applies as well to the former, "tough to define but impossible to confuse" (*Singer's Typewriter* 161). Dispelling any confusion over the fact that he is Jewish, Stavans sees his outsider/insider status as an extension of his Jewishness. "To be Jewish," he proclaims, "is to have a sense of otherness, to be at once an insider and an outsider" (109).

Stavans is both a secularist and a skeptic, and his outsider/insider ambivalence extends to Jewishness itself. For all the importance that he repeatedly places on his own ethnic background, he is highly critical of what he considers the insularity of a Mexican Jewish community he calls "as bizarre as unicorns" (248) as well as of Israeli belligerence. He frequently denounces the complacency, materialism, and provincialism of the "frighteningly monolingual" (292) American Jews who, overwhelmingly Ashkenazi, remain Eurocentric, nostalgic for vanished shtetls, and oblivious to Sephardi traditions.

Nevertheless, he is unmistakably Jewish, not least in his Talmudic propensity to quibble with other Jews. His favorite syntactic structure, like the *pilpul* of Talmud scholars, is the question, "La vida es una serie de preguntas sin repuesta" (Stavans and Zurita 14), he maintains—Life is a series of questions without response. His favorite Jewish philosopher is the ostracized rationalist Baruch Spinoza. In a conversation with Justin David, the rabbi of Congregation B'nai Israel in Northampton, Massachusetts, Stavans explains how his skepticism toward everything, including Judaism, makes him particularly Jewish: "So why do I endorse a skeptical approach? Because it defines my way of relating to the universe. Everything that comes to me—everything that is filtered through my mind—needs to be questioned. The questioning is an end [in] itself, for it doesn't lead to either certainty or denial. I'm convinced this is a Jewish attitude, by the way. What does the Talmud want from us if not to argue? To argue about everything: about God, about morality, about existence, even about the value of argument" (Stavans and David). Only a Jew would argue with that.

In his memoir *On Borrowed Words* (2001), Stavans is repulsed by the proselytizing Hasidim who "kidnap" him in Jerusalem and sequester him for a few intensive days in a yeshiva. He situates himself, uncomfortably, at the midpoint of a spectrum between Orthodoxy and assimilation. Contending that Jewishness does not require observance of Judaism, he maintains that "para ser judío, no es necesario creer en Dios" (Stavans and Zurita 43)—to be a Jew, it is not necessary to believe in God. And, in fact, Stavans calls God "another superstition" (Stavans and Jakšić 125), like nationalism. Nevertheless, in at least one book, *Ilan Stavans: Eight Conversations* (Sokol), he consistently observes the Orthodox taboo against writing out the full name of the Deity, preferring instead to spell it "G-d." And, elsewhere, he states: "I'm a weak believer, although I'm not an unbeliever" (Stavans and Gracia 53) and that "I do believe in God, albeit with a high degree of skepticism" (*Singer's Typewriter* 131). He believes that the Torah portrays the Deity as a rich but repellent personality: "There is no sugar coating it," he declares: "the biblical God is a warmonger" (Stavans and Page).

Nevertheless, just as his disdain for nationalism did not prevent him from serving in the Mexican Army and later becoming a naturalized citizen of the United States, Stavans's skepticism about God did not prevent him from producing the *New World Haggadah* (2016), though it is an unconventional, multilingual, multicultural text for conducting a Passover seder. It does not prevent him from treating God as a nettlesome personality he can quarrel with. Much of *With All Thine Heart* (2010) consists of attempts by Stavans and his interlocutor, Mordecai Drache, to make sense of the shape-shifting, moody Being who appears throughout the Hebrew Bible. Nor does Stavans's skepticism prevent him from occasionally going to synagogue: "I need ritual," he explains. "I also need community. And I need to find a place where I can comfortably express my doubts" (*Singer's Typewriter* 132). Stavans's theology positions him closer to Spinoza than Maimonides: "I believe in a godhead, capricious and unconcerned with earthly affairs" (Sokol 168).

Stavans concludes his youthful sojourn in a bellicose Israel "shaped by a besieged mentality" (*On Borrowed Words* 197) by returning to North America and resigning himself to being a Diaspora Jew, which is to say a Jew at odds with the centrality of Jewishness, if not his own Jewish identity. He is a modern, attentive but nonobservant wandering Jew who nevertheless gave his two sons the ancient Hebraic names Joshua and Isaiah. "I am a secular Jew interested in global culture" ("On Self-Translation"), he explains. As his "idols" (*One-Handed Pianist* 181), he names Baruch Spinoza—who was excommunicated from the Talmud Torah congregation of Amsterdam and who, he says, "along with Socrates, is in my view the most admirable of Westerns thinkers" (*With All Thine Heart* 12)—and Franz Kafka—who famously wrote in a January 8, 1914, diary entry: "What have I in common with Jews? I have hardly anything in common with myself and should stand very quietly in a corner, content that I can breathe" (252). Stavans paints himself as the quintessential Jew precisely because he is an anomaly.

The Yiddish writer he has chosen to edit and champion—through three volumes of his collected short stories and a volume of photographs, all published by the Library of America—is Isaac Bashevis Singer, whose erotically charged tales of demons and fanatics are as unorthodox—and unOrthodox—as Stavans. Though his father was a Hasidic rabbi, Singer rejected traditional religious observance in favor of a kind of Spinozistic pantheism that put him, like Spinoza, at odds with normative Judaism. In 1978, when he became the only Yiddish author ever to receive the Nobel Prize in Literature, Singer aroused the resentment of many who regarded him as a charlatan, unworthy to be honored throughout the world as the final embodiment

The Restless Ilan Stavans

of Yiddishkeit. "I profoundly despise him," snarled Inna Grade, embittered over the relative neglect suffered by her late husband, Chaim. "I am very sorry that America is celebrating the blasphemous buffoon" (Newhouse). Allan Nadler, the director of Jewish Studies at Drew University, was even more pointed: "When Abraham Sutzkever was starving, fighting Nazis with the partisans in the Lithuanian woods and writing great Yiddish poetry about the tragic fate of the Jews on fragments of bark, Singer was eating cheese blintzes at Famous Dairy Restaurant on 72nd Street and thinking about Polish whores and Yiddish devils" (Newhouse). Singer's status as an outsider within the Yiddish literary community is surely part of the reason Stavans chose to begin writing a biography of him.

Like Bernard Malamud, a significant Jewish writer who—unaccountably, especially given the Yiddish coloration of Malamud's fiction—has eluded his attention, Stavans employs the figure of the Jew as a metaphor. "And isn't Jewishness an essential feature of European modernity?" he asks (*The Scroll and the Cross* 7). And, to Stavans, no Jew was more modern than Harry Houdini (né Ehrich Weiss), the plucky immigrant from Hungary who used his magic to transform himself into "a superhero, a symbol of interwar Diaspora Jews" (*Singer's Typewriter* 51). Houdini was a role model to his adoring Jewish public "because he was simultaneously an insider and an outsider" (52). At once an insider and an outsider is of course the way that Stavans sees himself and the way he delineates his role as cultural commentator. As a light-skinned Jew, he does not conform to the common image of a Mexican or a Latino. And as a Latino who is at least ambivalent about traditions of worship, he is as Jewish as Spinoza and Kafka. But he is uniquely positioned to be a secular midrashist to both Latino and Jewish cultures, as well as to function as an emissary between the two. He was able to serve on both Massachusetts governor Deval Patrick's Latino American Affairs Commission and the board of the National Yiddish Book Center, to edit both *The Oxford Book of Latin American Essays* (1997) and *The Oxford Book of Jewish Stories* (1998).

Because of their migratory history as involuntary outsiders, Diaspora Jews—cosmopolitan and polyglot by necessity—have been traders and translators. Early in the twentieth century, when Yiddish and Hebrew competed for the allegiance of Jewish writers, the Yiddish critic Israel Isidor Elyashev, who wrote under the nom de plume Baal-Makhshoves, insisted that "from its inception our literature has nearly always been a *bilingual* one" (Baal-Makhshoves 107). A full accounting of all the languages in addition to Hebrew and Yiddish (Aramaic, English, French, German, Greek, Hungarian, Italian, Ladino, Latin, Polish, Portuguese, Russian, Serbian, Spanish, etc.) in which Jews have written would mock *bi*lingual as an understatement. So what Stavans has to say about Jewish literature is true not only for contemporary times: "Polyglotism is a permanent birthmark in the modern Jewish literary tradition, an unequivocal sign of the times" (*Inveterate Dreamer* 9).

For two millennia, it was Jews who brought in goods and words from other lands. So, too, does quadrilingual Stavans participate in the import-export business of ideas. He is most unabashedly Jewish not when he is davening but when he proclaims: "To be Jewish is to serve as a bridge between cultures" (*Singer's Typewriter* 109). Stavans is confident that "Jews will continue to act as conduits—a bridge between cultures" (*Inveterate Dreamer* 28), and that he will be the Allenby Bridge between Jews, between Latinos, between Jews and Latinos, and between Jews and Latinos and everyone else. In a twenty-page review of *Latino USA* that testifies to Stavans's stature, Paul Allatson takes issue with his pontifications (i.e., bridgings) as centered on his own experiences and interests and oblivious to others, contending that the portrait of Latinos that Stavans paints is a portrait of himself: "Stavans's self-appointed bridging function is presented as if no other Mexican or 'American,' Latino or otherwise, has ever attempted a dialogue, or indeed attempted to do the comic work that *Latino USA* purports to do" (Allatson 37).

Nevertheless, Stavans was the natural choice to edit *Oy, Caramba! An Anthology of Jewish Stories from Latin America* (2016), *The Scroll and the Cross: 1,000 Years of Jewish-Hispanic Literature* (2003), and *Tropical Synagogues: Short Stories by Jewish-Latin American Writers* (1994) as well as a series of books by Twentieth-Century Latin American Jewish Women Writers for the University of New Mexico Press (1997–2006). He devoted an entire book, *Borges, the Jew* (2016), to the Gentile Argentine's affinity with Jews, and much of *Imagining Columbus: The Literary Voyage* (1993) is spent imagining how the Genoese explorer might in fact have been a crypto-Jew. His Jewish and Latino backgrounds came together again in *Once@9:53*, a fotonovela about the devastating July 18, 1994, bomb attack on AMIA—the Asociación Mutuel Israelita Argentina in Buenos Aires—that he created with photographer Marcelo Brodsky. The perfect metonymy for Ilan Stavans as Hispanic Jew is the recipe for *Latkes con Mole* that he published in *Singer's Typewriter and Mine* (233–34). In a lecture at the U.S. Holocaust Museum and an essay published in *A Critic's Journey* (77–84), he was able to speak with special authority about "Hispanic Anti-Semitism," identifying three distinct modalities to the phenomenon: Catholic, ideological, and anti-Zionist.

Furthermore, Stavans, who has translated Jorge Luis Borges, Oscar Hahn, Pablo Neruda, and Juan Rulfo into English, Elizabeth Bishop, Emily Dickinson, and Cynthia Ozick into Spanish, Isaac Bashevis Singer from Yiddish, Yehuda Halevi and Yehuda Amichai from Hebrew, and parts of *Don Quixote* and *Hamlet* into Spanglish, sees translators, like Jews, as quintessential outsider-insiders: "They are in the know in regard to a social group, but their capacity to speak to another turns them into bridges" (Stavans and Ellison 65). He affirms his ethnic kinship with such prominent translators as J. M. Cohen, John Felstiner, Mirra Ginsburg, Howard Goldblatt, Edith Grossman, Michael Hamburger, Richard Howard, Curt Leviant, Suzanne Jill

Levine, Joachim Neugroschel, Robert Pinsky, Burton Raffel, David R. Slavitt, and Eliot Weinberger. Stavans's activities as a translator even extend into languages he does not speak. Working with Gvantsa Jobava, a native of Tbilisi who is deputy chair of the Georgian Publishers and Booksellers Association, he Englished a poem, "Digging Out Potatoes," by the Georgian poet Besik Kharanauli (Kharanauli).

As in his discussions of Hispanic matters, Stavans often poses as a spokesperson for the Jewish community, employing the pronoun "we" for his commentaries on Jewish themes. "Yes, at the core we secular Jews," he proclaims, "often described as the role models of modernity, pretend to be like everyone else, maybe even better: we pretend to be like everyone else while at the same time seek to retain a degree of uniqueness" (*Singer's Typewriter* 162). He is thus contending that Jews themselves are both insiders—"the role models of modernity"—and outsiders—retaining "a degree of uniqueness." But he presents himself as both an outsider and an insider to that outsider/insider Jewish culture. A native speaker of Yiddish who proclaims, awkwardly, "I love Hebrew profusely" ("Dying in Hebrew" 604), he is drawn again and again to Jewish themes, from Genesis to *Seinfeld*. (The adverb makes another clumsy appearance when he discusses saxophonist Paquito D'Rivera "whose music I admire profusely" (Foreword to *My Sax Life* vii)). However, Stavans also reports that he has allowed his command of Hebrew to atrophy, that he abandoned his attempt at *aliyah*, and that he finds the American Jewish community stiflingly insular.

The writer who declares that "literature is about pleasure, whereas religion is about fear" (*Knowledge and Censorship* 113) is a renegade, certainly not a *yeshiva bokher*, or even a nice Jewish boy. But then, again, the lessons of Jewish narrative from Adam through Alexander Portnoy is that "nice Jewish boys" also harbor the instincts of an outlaw. The reason Stavans felt uncomfortable in Israel is that Jews there are in the majority. "I enjoyed then—and I enjoy now," he explains, "being in the minority" (Sokol 15). And cultural critic is itself a minority occupation.

5 THE MULTICULTURAL MOMENT

> When you come to the fork in the road, take it.
> —Yogi Berra (qtd. in Barra xxxv)

Stavans's ascension to the role of prominent public intellectual, his stardom, must be understood as a function of the multicultural moment in which it occurred. It was, by his own account, "the moment when multiculturalism was in vogue and there were heated debates on bilingual education, affirmative action, and the shaping of the Western canon" (*Critic's Journey* 195). *Diversity* was the favored nonce word. Just as he is able to describe himself as an "accidental Mexican," because his grandparents arrived at the port of Veracruz not out of any particular attraction to Mexico but because that country happened to be hospitable to Eastern Europe immigrants at a time when the United States was not, it is possible to imagine a distinctly different career if he had emigrated a decade or two earlier or a decade or two later.

By 1985, the year in which Stavans arrived in New York, perhaps the most ethnically diverse of North American cities, "ethnic literature" was already an acceptable and popular category of study. The old canon of white European Christian male authors had been successfully challenged, and high school and college curricula and popular best-seller lists were now including works by outsiders such as James Baldwin, Saul Bellow, Ralph Ellison, Bernard Malamud, Toni Morrison, and Philip Roth. Alex Haley's novel *Roots: The Saga of an American Family* spent twenty-two weeks atop the best-seller lists after its publication in 1976, and its adaptation as an ABC-TV miniseries in 1977 set records for viewership and dramatically altered public understanding of what constitutes "an American family." Woody Allen, Mel Brooks, and Neil Simon made Jewish characters familiar to Gentiles. *Holocaust*, the melodramatic miniseries broadcast in four parts in 1978, brought Jewish suffering into millions of American—and German—homes.

Latino culture trailed African American and Jewish cultures in penetrating into the mainstream, but 1990, when Oscar Hijuelos became the first U.S.-born Hispanic to win the Pulitzer Prize for Fiction, for his novel *The Mambo Kings Play Songs of Love*, marked a turning point. It was the year in which Stavans earned a doctorate from Columbia University and entered the academic job market. Julia Alvarez, Sandra Cisneros, and Cristina García were gaining wide readerships, while salsa was well on its way to surpassing ketchup as the most popular condiment on American tables. Stavans in fact dismisses Cisneros as an opportunist whose "works are pamphleteering. They denounce rather than move; they accuse rather than educate" (*Riddle of Cantínflas* 115). He attributes her broad critical and popular success less to her talent, which he considers modest, than to the fact that she came along at a time when the culture demanded a Latina literary celebrity: "By the late eighties, multiculturalism had become a national obsession, and a spokesfigure for the brewing Latino minority was urgently needed" (83). A decade later, just as Latinos were about to outnumber African Americans as the nation's largest ethnic minority and were increasingly asserting their economic, political, and cultural clout, the academy was also ready to anoint an interpreter of these multicultural developments. Poised to be the voice of the Latino ascendancy, Stavans would devote much of his energy to championing the increased influence of Latinos on the politics, music, and food of the United States.

After the University of California at Berkeley established the nation's first department of ethnic studies, in 1969, dozens of other institutions followed suit. The need to staff these programs as well as new affirmative action initiatives to hire nontraditional faculty created an acute demand. By 1993 (when Steven Spielberg's *Schindler's List* was released), Stavans was a junior faculty member at Bernard M. Baruch College, a former business school that had only recently, in 1968, been reorganized as a senior unit of the mammoth City University of New York. New York City itself had barely survived economic collapse and was continuing to experience high rates of crime. The number of violent crimes and murders for the New York metropolitan area peaked at 212,458 and 2,605, respectively, in 1990 ("New York Crime"). With new budget constraints, the city's public university system was challenged by controversies over free tuition and open enrollment. Like a deus ex machina, a Cinderella offer rescued Stavans from urban academic drudgery, instantly transforming an obscure assistant professor at Baruch College into a full professor at idyllic and prestigious Amherst College, a highly selective, expensive liberal arts college located in a small town in the scenic Pioneer Valley. He would be teaching at the alma mater of such quintessential Yankees as Calvin Coolidge, Henry Clay Folger, and Harlan Fiske Stone. Seven years after his arrival in 1993, Amherst would bestow on him the august title Lewis-Sebring Professor in Latin American and Latino Culture.

Stavans's talent and industriousness surely had much to do with his sudden metamorphosis. But so did timing. An articulate Latino Jew who champions diversity and works to bridge cultures, Stavans seemed a perfect embodiment of the fin-de-siècle zeitgeist. He came to Amherst with a clear and timely agenda: "I feel that there is a job that is clamoring to be done: to investigate the crossroads where Jews and Hispanics come together, not only today but yesterday and tomorrow" (Sokol 61). The Mexican-Jewish immigrant professor added an element of "diversity" to a relatively homogeneous campus that had only recently, in 1969, created its Black Studies Department and, in 1975, become coeducational. Harvard University had recruited Henry Louis Gates Jr. to its faculty in 1991, and Amherst was counting on the prestige it, too, would gain by hiring an increasingly prominent public intellectual; it was also counting on their unusual newcomer to be a role model to students, faculty, and staff. Nevertheless, Stavans would later level sharp criticism at identity politics. A proud citizen of the world, he is impatient with the multicultural tribalism that encouraged his own ascendancy. "Ours is a fractured, discombobulated society," he complains. "In the United States—Blacks, Jews, Asians, Latinos, gays, and this and that. So everybody has their own little representative and nobody listens to anybody else" (Sokol 72).

Instead, especially in his book *The United States of Mestizo*, Stavans celebrates *mestizaje* and makes frequent reference to the ideal promulgated by José Vasconcelos, often called the "cultural caudillo of the Mexican Revolution," of *la raza cósmica*, the supreme amalgam of all ethnicities that will create the Universópolis and inaugurate the *"era universal de la humanidad."* Heralding "the arrival of a new underclass: the mestizo proletariat" (Stavans and Jakšić 68), Stavans's celebration of mixing is also a revolutionary assault on a rigid social hierarchy that arrogates privilege to the "pure." Though comfortably middle class, he aligns himself with the "proletarian" vanguard of a future in which separate categories are dissolved and all races and ethnicities blend.

Such cultural miscegenation puts Stavans at odds with the impulse toward ethnic separatism out of which many of the institutional structures from which he personally benefited arose. Defining *mestizaje* as, above all, "a state of mind," he proclaims that "by virtue of cross-fertilization defining the world in its entirety, we're all mestizos now, no matter if one comes from Managua, Cairo, or Seoul" (*United States of Mestizo* 36). Although the ugly history of laws prohibiting interracial marriage and other forms of racial mixing in the United States has endowed the word *miscegenation* with negative connotations, Stavans celebrates it. Alloys are stronger than their components. "If W. E. B. DuBois argued that the 20th century was about the color line," he declares, "my intuition (and there is plenty of evidence already) is that the 21st century will be about miscegenation" (*Latinos in the United States* xxvii). If, however, mixing is this century's mode, does it make sense to cluster separately as Latinos and Jews, the very labels that have been the engines of Stavans's career?

Moreover, he is keenly aware of the contingency of that career. In *On Borrowed*

Words, he explains to Richard Rodriguez the organizing principle behind the memoir: "In retrospect, life appears to be full of meaning. But only in retrospect, since the meaning is not usually understood as events unfold, because the sole guiding force shaping our existence is chance. Nothing more, nothing less than Darwinian accidents make us the people that we are" (248). Among the Darwinian accidents that account for Ilan Stavans, author of *On Borrowed Words*, is his birth in Mexico City, a product of restrictive immigration laws in the United States rather than any particular desire on the part of his grandparents to strike roots as Chilangos. "By accident," he acknowledges, "I'm a Spanish speaker" (Wassner 492). In his long poem *The Wall*, he declares: "I / could / have been born / in Israel, / in South Africa, / in West Germany, / in New York, / but / I was born / in / Mexico City / into / a / civilization / that / turns / resignation / into / grit" (82–83).

Stavans and his wife Alison visited Auschwitz on their honeymoon, and he remains acutely aware that if his grandmother had not made her way to North America, she would have met the same fate as her sisters: extermination. "¿Por qué soy yo el que está vivo y no uno de tantos nietos des las hermanas de mi abuela?" he, a survivor—unlike the grandchildren of his grandmother's sisters—wonders. "¿Qué coincidencias se articularon para que yo pudiera escribir estas líneas?" (Stavans and Zurita 29). He marvels over the concatenation of happenstances that played out to enable him to avoid the Holocaust and write those lines. Stavans's vision of life as a garden of forking paths—and of God as capricious and inscrutable—was surely shaped or at least reinforced by his own fortuitous trajectory. He understands how, beginning with the "sheer chance" of his grandparents' relocation in Mexico (*Inveterate Dreamer* 253), his life might have turned out quite differently. He can thus proclaim: "I look at the world as a theater of accidents" (Stavans and Gracia 101).

A view of experience as aleatory is behind ¡*Lotería!* (2004), his study of the Mexican national lottery and other games of chance. He notes that his own grandfather, Zeyde Srulek, a pesoless immigrant from the Ukraine, bought a winning lottery ticket that immediately changed his life. "Every single decision we make," Stavans concludes, "no matter how insignificant, represents a forking path before us. To choose one alternative among many is to say no to the other ones—to say no to the other selves we might have been" (¡*Lotería!* xxi). Had Stavans's grandparents been able to immigrate to New York or Boston or Philadelphia, he might have turned out to be just another native-born American Jew. "How different would my life be had my ancestors not immigrated from Poland and the Ukraine to Mexico but to Johannesburg or Shanghai?" (Stavans and Gracia 188), he asks. Had his application to Mexico's Centro Universitario de Estudios Cinematográficos not been rejected, he might have been able to follow his first love, film, and not become a literary critic at all. Or, rather, his second love, since he writes in *Latino USA*: "I dreamed, from early on, of becoming first a graphic artist, and then a filmmaker" (x). Instead of becoming an author, he might have ended up like Roberto Weil, creating the artwork accompanying the text that someone else provided in the graphic novel *Mr. Spic Goes to Washington* (2008).

"A man's life is filled with unexpected twists and turns which shape his destiny" (*Gabriel García Márquez* 181), Stavans observes about the quirky shifts in the life of Gabriel García Márquez and about the possibility that *One Hundred Years of Solitude* might never have come to be written. He himself might never have written his book on García Márquez's early years had he not devoured the Colombian's most famous novel during one rainy day in Mexico City. A passionate reader, Stavans insists that even a bibliophile's exposure to books is haphazard: "Es el azar quien ordena nuestra lectures" (*Prontuario* 19)—It is chance that determines what we read. Seizing on travel as most illustrative of the adventitiousness of the human condition, Stavans and coauthor Joshua Ellison declare that "there is a felicity of mind that comes with a strong sense of life's basic contingency; these are qualities that engender irony, audacity, and improvisation" (12). Irony, audacity, and improvisation could be ascribed to Stavans's own writing, as well as to the way he has seized the moment throughout his career.

As with individual lives and travel, Stavans believes that history in general is a concatenation of contingencies: through a consistent insistence on the inconsistency of history, which he likens to a kaleidoscope, Stavans's conception of the span of human experience as "neverending flux" (*Latino USA* 12) would sabotage the entire project of formulating meaningful historical narrative. The most a conscientious historian could say is: This happened and then that happened and then that happened and then . . . However, though playfully and proudly contrarian, Stavans is a polemicist, and though his two comic histories—*A Most Imperfect Union* and *Latino USA*—are breezy, sweeping, carnivalesque blends of high and low, they are not concessions of aporia. They possess purpose and design, even if the anonymous reviewer for *Publishers Weekly* described the former as "a random smattering of disparaging comments" (*Publishers Weekly*). The objective that he posits for the latter, "to represent Hispanic civilization as a fiesta of types, archetypes, and stereotypes" (*Latino USA* xv), presupposes patterns in culture. Though an individual life is as much a concatenation of contingencies as is the broad sweep of history, publication of *The Essential Ilan Stavans* in 2000 and of the autobiography *On Borrowed Words* in 2001 presumed that its subject possesses a core identity, that there *is* an essence to Ilan Stavans.

A belief in the reality of types, archetypes, and stereotypes constitutes a rejection of history as merely inchoate, uninstructive flux. "At the heart of the nineteenth century is a central concept: Progress" (*Most Imperfect Union* 105), Stavans declares, absolutely, brooking no doubt. Later, he states, unequivocally, that "salvation has always been the core of the American religious enterprise" (221). He often presents himself as a thoroughgoing relativist; invoking Giambattista Vico, "the father of historical perspectivism" (*Love & Language* 5), he instead calls himself a "perspectivist" (4). However, a sincere believer that "history is nothing but a sideboard of possibilities" (3), that things could always have turned out other than they did, and that truth is a function of perception, could not, with unwavering confidence, proclaim that slavery is "the morally bankrupt domination of one race over another" (*Most Imperfect Union* 27) or, after recounting the Treaty of Guadalupe Hidalgo, which resulted in the sale of two-thirds of Mexico to the United States for $15 million, inject the sardonic opinion: "What a steal" (*Latino USA* 35). If all is chance, judgment is pointless.

So, too, might writing be. A meditation on the incipient dementia of his aging father leads Stavans to ponder the fragility and facticity of memory. "Memory is a stage with an unfolding play whose entire cast is invented," he declares ("Friday Takeaway: Forgetting"). If the self is a construct of fleeting memories and memories are a convenient fiction, personal identity becomes a mere chimera. A keen memory is a crucial asset for a professional actor, but, observing Abraham Stavchansky forget even what he said a minute before, Stavans reflects on the vanity of human wishes. He often espouses a belief in immortality through art, that the writing outlives the writer, proclaiming elsewhere that he writes in order to defy mortality. However, the spectacle of his father's mental entropy leads the prolific author to radical skepticism about the survival—if not the value—of what he writes. "When young," writes Stavans, "I wanted to be remembered, thinking that memory was synonymous with success. Now that I see my name on a book cover or hear references to my name on the radio, the feeling I get is of fatuousness. I know that everything I do—including these words—will be forgotten, as it should. What survives, at best, is an echo" ("Friday Takeaway: Forgetting"). Stavans becomes the fading echo of the faint plaint of Ozymandias.

6 THE IMMIGRANT MELT

> My family didn't cross the border,
> the border crossed us.
>
> —Eva Longoria

When Eva Longoria, a ninth-generation American born in Corpus Christi, Texas, uttered those words, on July 25, 2016, at the Democratic National Convention in Philadelphia, she was echoing a familiar slogan of Chicano activists. As spoils of a war it won in 1848, the United States appropriated for itself about half the sovereign territory of Mexico. The Spanish-speaking inhabitants of what are now Arizona, California, Nevada, Texas, Utah and parts of Colorado, New Mexico, and Wyoming suddenly found themselves incorporated into a largely English-speaking society. Their nationality changed, though they had not moved. They were not immigrants.

Stavans, though, *is* an immigrant. A native of Mexico City, he became a naturalized citizen of the United States, technically, a Mexican American—just as, though white, Elon Musk, who was born in Pretoria, is an African American. However, as some of his critics pointedly observe, Stavans is not a Chicano. He crossed the border, and the border did not cross him. Not only is Stavans an immigrant; immigration is a subject to which he has returned again and again. He has offered several poignant accounts of his first months in New York, when, a stranger in a strange land, he wandered about, tongue-tied, lonely, and confused. But he has also described the exhilarating freedom of being able to forge a fresh identity in a free and hospitable society. More generally, he has acknowledged the hardships faced by any immigrant—"the loss of language; the loss of identity, the loss of self-esteem; and, more important, the loss of tradition" (*Hispanic Condition* 18). However, while noting that some greenhorns are decisively defeated by the obstacles they face, he is generally sanguine about immigration to the United States: "In this nation of imagination and plenty, where newcomers are welcome to reinvent their past, loss quickly becomes an asset" (18). Nevertheless, Stavans makes frequent enough reference to his belief that home is not a place but a language and that movement, not arrival, is the natural state for sentient life to complicate his picture of immigration. Moreover, he retained his Mexican citizenship even after "becoming American."

The ordeal of trying to adapt to another country remained crucial enough to Stavans that, fourteen years after his arrival in New York, he undertook the ambitious project of putting together an anthology of immigrant writing, and he included within it an excerpt from his own autobiography, *On Borrowed Words*. Published by the Library of America, *Becoming Americans: Four Centuries of Immigrant Writing* (2009) includes texts—memoirs, travelogues, fiction, poetry—by eighty-five authors from the fifteenth century to the present. Stavans chooses to begin his formidable lineup with Christopher Columbus, who died sixty-two years before what the *Oxford English Dictionary* records as the first appearance of the word *American*. Moreover, Columbus never became American, in the sense of a resident of what is now the United States. He never set foot on any parcel of land that is now within its borders. And, though he traveled to Africa and the Western Hemisphere, he was born in Europe and died in Europe. He was an explorer, not an immigrant.

So what is Stavans's powerful attraction to Cristóbal Colón, a Genoan who made his famous voyages under a Spanish flag? Enduring childhood fascination with the controversial explorer inspired Stavans to write his first book, *Imagining Columbus: The Literary Voyage* (1993), a study that begins with the premise that "Columbus is, for the most part, whatever people want him to be" (xii). During the quincentennial of Columbus's first voyage, when Stavans was writing the book, Italian Americans continued to use the explorer as a rallying point for ethnic pride. However, American Indian activists wanted Columbus to be seen not as a daring, farsighted navigator but as the vainglorious epitome of genocidal European imperialism. "He personifies courage and glory but also death and destruction" (xvii–xviii), says Stavans, attempting to balance contrasting views of Columbus. A movement was afoot to rename and rededicate what the United States calls Columbus Day—Día de la Raza in much of Latin America—as Indigenous Peoples' Day. So, at the beginning of his career, Stavans was already functioning as a public intellectual, confronting contemporary controversy. The uncorroborated legend that Columbus was a crypto-Jew and that his interpreter, Luis de Torres, spoke Hebrew to the indigenous people they met during their first landfall, in San Salvador, must have been an added lagniappe for Stavans, a scholar of the endangered Jews who tried to survive the Inquisition by converting to Christianity or pretending to convert.

The anthology follows the selections from Columbus's journals with an excerpt from Álvar Núñez Cabeza de Vaca's *Chronicle of the Narváez Expedition*. Earlier, in the Introduction to a 2002 edition of the complete book, Stavans had described the hapless conquistador's wanderings—naked, famished, and lost—from Florida to New Mexico as "a Dantean pilgrimage through the chambers of hell and purgatory" (Introduction to *Chronicle of the Narváez Expedition* x). Like Columbus, Cabeza de Vaca, who died in Seville two centuries before the founding of the United States, was neither an immigrant nor an example of "Becoming American." Also an uncomfortable fit in the volume is Charles Chaplin, a native of England who never applied for U.S. citizenship and, after being hounded by the House Un-American Activities Committee, which did not see him as "becoming American," spent the last twenty-five years of his life in Switzerland. In addition, although he did become a citizen of the nation that gave him refuge, it might be more accurate to term Thomas Mann an *exile* than an *immigrant*; after the fall of the Nazi regime that he had fled, Mann returned to Europe for the rest of his life. Moreover, *immigrant* also seems an odd word to apply to at least two other authors in the collection, Phillis Wheatley and Ayuba Suleiman Diallo, who were abducted from Africa and brought involuntarily to North America, as slaves. So, even in his later book *Words in Transit: Stories of Immigrants* (2016), a collection of interviews with foreigners who have moved to western Massachusetts and are in various stages of "becoming American," Stavans is more interested in the enigmas of arrival, the upheaval of movement, than in the process of naturalization. He is a diasporist more drawn to the challenges and rewards of dislocation than to the anesthetizing comforts of settlement.

Stavans's career coincides with a tidal wave of immigration to the United States. Its impact rivals that of the tsunami of more than 20 million newcomers that broke over the East Coast between 1880 and 1914, a time when the total population of the United States was barely 75 million. In 1907, the peak year for immigration to the United States and the year in which Henry Roth's *Call It Sleep* (1934), a touchstone for Stavans's discussions of American Jewish culture, begins, 1,285,350 newcomers passed through Ellis Island. The immigrants, mostly from Europe, included the forebears of the American Jews among whom Stavans, also descended from displaced Ashkenazi Jews, is an uneasy fit. World War I and nativist xenophobia led to the passage in 1923 of the Johnson–Reed Act, which barred entry to most immigrants from Eastern and Southern Europe. Stavans's grandparents left Eastern Europe after the doors to the United States had already been closed to their kind, and they had to settle for settling in Mexico instead.

In 1910, 14.7 percent of Americans were foreign-born, but by 1970 that proportion had dwindled to 4.7 percent. However, the liberalized Immigration Act of 1990 coupled with economic hardship and political violence abroad led to more than one million immigrants during each subsequent year. By 2015, the share of foreign-born in the U.S. population had jumped to 13.5 percent (Zong and Batalova). While most of the immigration a century earlier had come from Eastern and Southern Europe, most of the new immigration was from Asia and Latin America—including, and especially, Stavans's native Mexico. "America must be kept American," declared

President Calvin Coolidge when signing the Johnson–Reed Act on December 26, 1923. A similar mistrust of outsiders gained momentum after the terrorist attacks against New York and Washington on September 11, 2001. Reviving the discredited 1930s isolationist slogan "America First," Donald J. Trump was elected president on a pledge to keep dangerous strangers—especially Muslim migrants—out of the United States, deport millions of aliens, and build a wall across the entire length of the 1,954-mile border with Mexico. At the same time, hundreds of thousands of refugees, fleeing violence and destitution in Syria, Eritrea, Somalia, Afghanistan, and other troubled countries, were being turned back at the borders of European nations.

Not surprisingly, Stavans was increasingly concerned about the growing hostility toward outsiders and minorities. In an op-ed piece published in the *New York Times* shortly after the Trump inauguration, he accused the new president of antipathy toward Latinos. He noted the failure to appoint Latinos to prominent positions in the new administration as well as Trump's continuing characterization of Mexico as "a nest of criminals." Observing that Trump "appears to be allergic to foreign languages, especially Spanish," he denounced him for expunging the Spanish section from the official White House website and saluted *español* as "a tool of defiance" ("Trump, the Wall and the Spanish Language"). By June 1, 2017, Stavans was tweeting a mock dictionary entry that oozes with contempt for the president: "'Trump, The,' Eng. noun. Slang for idiotic nightmare. First usage: Nov. 2016. 'Trumping,' Verb. Tripping on one's stupidity."

Long before the ascendancy of Trump caused him to worry about the rise in bigotry and intolerance, Stavans posited a correlation between political freedom and the quality of thought. In his Introduction to *The Oxford Book of Latin American Essays*, he reflects on why the genre of reflective essay has been marginal in a region characterized by military dictatorships. "Let me invoke the word *democracy* at this point," he says, "for democracy and critical thinking go hand in hand. One cannot live without the other; one depends on the other not only to survive but to thrive" (4). The claim that critical thinking is impossible without democracy is refuted by the examples of Galileo, Isaac Newton, Voltaire, Andrei Sakharov, and Fang Lizhi, all of whom managed to think freely within societies not close to being democratic. Later, Stavans qualifies his generalization by admitting that "Latin America is filled with critical thinkers, but they are by definition outcasts" (5). Because critical thinking is perceived as a threat to conventional wisdom even—and especially—in a democracy, critical thinkers are peripheral figures, even outcasts, everywhere. Stavans delights in performing the role of critical thinker.

In 2016, his publishing company established the Restless Books Prize for New Immigrant Writing, an annual competition for book-length manuscripts by first-time authors who are first-generation residents of their country. The prize is $10,000 and publication by Restless Books. "In these times of intense xenopho-bia," explained the publisher, Stavans, "it is more important than ever that these boundary-crossing stories reach the broadest possible audience." The inaugu-ral recipient of the prize, Deepak Unnikrishnan's *Temporary People*, is a series of twenty-eight linked stories about foreign workers in the United Arab Emirates. Its author moved to the United States from Abu Dhabi. Erecting his own preoccu-pations into a hyperbolic precept, he declared: "The ethos of the modern world is defined by immigrants" (Restless Books Prize). In 2017, the Restless Books Prize went to Grace Talusan for *The Body Papers*, a memoir of her experiences as an un-documented immigrant whose parents brought her as a child with them from the Philippines to the United States. And the 2018 recipient was Priyanka Champaneri for *The City of Good Death*, a novel about the proprietor of a hostel in Benares, where Hindus come to die a holy death.

Immigration is central to Stavans's several discussions of Alberto Gerchunoff, a "magisterial figure" (*Oy, Caramba!* 8) in Jewish literature of Latin America and the first notable Jewish writer in centuries to use Spanish. Born, like Stavans, into a Yiddish-speaking family, Gerchunoff was seven in 1910 when they moved to Ar-gentina. By age twenty-six, he had mastered Spanish well enough to publish *Los gauchos judíos* (1910) (*The Jewish Gauchos of the Pampas*), a collection of linked sto-ries that, according to Stavans, are notable for "setting a linguistic and narrative standard" (*Oy, Caramba!* 8). He compares Gerchunoff to Conrad and Nabokov in his translingual brilliance, his success at writing exquisite prose in what was, after Yiddish and Russian, an adopted tongue. Stavans reads *Los gaucho judíos*—twenty-six stories about Jews who have adapted to the cattle culture of the Pampas—as the embodiment of a smitten immigrant's dream of Argentina as a pluralistic democra-cy: "Gerchunoff meant his text to be a celebration of the nation's friendly, tolerant, and multiethnic spirit" (*Oy, Caramba!* 11). However, he notes that less than a decade later, from January 7 to 14, 1919, the pogrom in Buenos Aires known as *la Semana Trágica* left hundreds of Jews dead. Over the years until his death in 1950, pervasive anti-Semitism shattered Gerchunoff's vision of Argentina as a free and open society into which a Jewish immigrant was welcome to assimilate. Yet to come were the Dirty War of the 1970s, in which Jews were particular targets and disproportionate victims, the bombing of the Israeli embassy in Buenos Aires in 1992, and the AMIA (Asociación Mutual Israelita Argentina) bombing in 1994 that left eighty-five dead and hundreds wounded.

Stavans finds in Ernesto Galarza's memoir, *Barrio Boy* (1971), a different version of immigration. Born in 1905, Galarza tells the story of how, as a child fleeing the Mexican Revolution with his family, he eventually makes his difficult way from Jal-cocotán, a mountain village in the state of Nayarit, to Sacramento, California. In his introduction to the fortieth anniversary edition of *Barrio Boy*, Stavans, whose background and experiences were quite different from Galarza's, presents the book as the quintessential American immigration story—"a Platonic universal, his odyssey a boilerplate that millions of other immigrants, Mexicans and otherwise, constantly replicated as they abandoned their places of origin somewhere in the so-called Third World in search of betterment" (xiii). It is a story of hardship but ultimately of fulfillment, as Galarza begins to grow into a resourceful, accomplished man capable of shaping his own life into articulate English, his adopted tongue. For much of his career as a scholar and activist, Galarza took issue with the theory—perhaps most provocatively advanced in "El pachuco y otros extremos," the opening chapter of Octavio Paz's book *El labertinto de la soledad* (1950) (*The Labyrinth of Solitude*)—that Chicanos suffered from a collective inferiority complex, arguing, instead, that for them assimilation to American society has been a process of addition rather than replacement. He rejected *malinchismo*—a word derived from La Malinche, the Nahua woman who became mistress to Hernán Cortés, to refer to a Mexican's self-hatred and attraction to the foreigner. When Galarza begins *Barrio Boy* by declaring: "This, then, is a true story of the acculturation of Little Ernie" (2), it is not with a sense of loss. Stavans contends that the book is addressed to a reader who is "Not an American per se but an *Americanized* person like Galarza himself, with an abundance of self-esteem, one capable of understanding what immigration as a story is all about" (Introduction to *Barrio Boy* xxiii).

Stavans is just such an Americanized reader, Galarza's ideal reader, and for him what immigration is all about is growth and complexity. That is of course a matter of immigration to the United States, not Argentina, the land of Gerchunoff's disenchantment, or Mexico, where Stavans's grandparents found a home but where he as a teenager felt compelled to join a Jewish self-defense militia. He attributed his difficulty in finding a publisher for his novella *Talia y el cielo* to Mexican anti-Semitism. As his reason for immigrating to the United States, he explains: "I came motivated by the desire to become a writer in a free, open society" (*Thirteen Ways* 127). "I love the United States," he says. "I'm grateful to it" (Stavans and Gracia 184). He emphasizes that gratitude in explaining his motivation for taking on an anthology of texts about the immigrant experience: "*Becoming Americans* is my love letter to the United States, a tolerant, warm-hearted country that has been extraordinarily generous to me as an immigrant. Among other things, the country has allowed me to explore my talents to the limit" (Kelley 9). Describing the experience of immigrants to the United States as a process of "reeducation not unlike the one I went through myself," he explains: "They adopt a set of values that includes everything: politics, yet, but also religion, health, music, fashion, cuisine" (*Knowledge and Censorship* 7). Again, Stavans' avidity for group identity leads him to dubious claims of shared traits; he has not adopted the Protestant religion of most other Americans, and it is unlikely that he shares their taste in pop music and fast food. Yet he is positively rhapsodic about the success of the American assimilationist model. "What fascinates me about the American experiment is that—lo and behold—it works!" (*Knowledge and Censorship* 7)," he wrote before the election of Donald J. Trump, whose nativist nationalism Stavans deplores.

Nevertheless, the fact that Stavans retained his Mexican citizenship after attaining naturalization in the United States suggests that his love for the latter has not been not unequivocal. As a writer, he has used his talents and the freedom he found north of the Rio Grande to question fundamental characteristics of his new nation as well as the very idea of national identity. *A Most Imperfect Union* is "contrarian" in its refusal to omit the ugly episodes of American history (slavery, genocide, exploitation of labor, foreign aggression, etc.) that more standard histories tend to ignore or minimize. Echoing the revisionism of Howard Zinn's *A People's History of the United States* (1980), he rejects the Hegelian "Great Man" theory of history and is less interested in the sculpted heads on Mount Rushmore than in the anonymous Americans and the slaveowners, robber barons, Indian-killers, militarists, and lynch mobs that have shaped the nation. Stavans even prefaces his book with a succinct catalog of the nation's imperfections: "its insatiable appetite for pleasure, its plastic-surgery aesthetics, its love of consumption, its frequent ignorance of history, its xenophobic disposition, its political correctness, its arrogant foreign policy" (*Most Imperfect Union* xi). Like Zinn and, later, Oliver Stone's television documentary *The Untold History of the United States* (2012), Stavans offers an alternative to the dominant triumphal narrative told about the land of the free and home of the brave. However, appealing to "contrarianism" as not only a polemical method but an ethical value as well, he also praises the United States for its toleration, even encouragement, of dissent: "Where else in the world does one have the freedom to contradict oneself?" he asks (*Most Imperfect Union* xv). Though he insists that "there is no art without anger" (*Art and Anger* x), he is, for the most part, a congenial contrarian.

His adversarial stance does not mean it is contradictory for Stavans to express his affection for a society that encourages the intellectual vitality he thrives on. He often ponders the Latin motto *e pluribus unum*—out of many, one—that is a translation into Enlightenment politics of ancient Greek philosophy's conundrum of trying to reconcile the One and the many. Which is more real, asked Plato and Aristotle, the forest or the trees? Does a forest have any reality of its own beyond the sum of the individual trees that comprise it? Can an individual tree be understood except within the context of a forest? Inscribed on the Great Seal of the United States at the suggestion of Swiss immigrant Pierre Eugène du Simitière, the phrase *e pluribus unum* was originally employed to refer to the fact that thirteen separate colonies were joining together to form a single, unified nation. However, it has since been taken as a recipe for cultural unity amid the multiplicity of the American populace—that the United States is an amalgam of a vast variety of races, religions, national origins, sexual orientations, and so on. It is a betrayal of that ideal either to suppress Latino (and, within it, Chicano, Puerto Rican, Cuban, Dominican) expression or allow it or any other monoculture—including the Anglo Saxon—to eclipse the others.

"The United States, a sum of units, is a pluralistic society," Stavans observes, unremarkably. "Pluralism is not only a political category but a cultural one too. It succeeds not by imposition but by consensus. A society such as ours, made up of numerous cultures, is invariably richer when those cultures are allowed to have their own space while, at the same time, communicating respectfully with the others" (Sokol 99–100). The challenge of "living in the hyphen" and "inhabiting the borderland" is in balancing *pluribus* with *unum*—achieving a national consensus without imposing uniformity and encouraging diversity without creating chaos. As an advocate of Latino and Jewish minorities and a champion of the contributions immigrants make to their new homeland, Stavans would seem partial to *pluribus*. However, he devoted an entire book, *The United States of Mestizo*, to proclaiming the values of hybridity and another, *Spanglish*, to defending the virtues of a mongrel tongue. In a blurb on the back cover of the former, Juan Felipe Herrera proclaims him "one of our major voices of *el nuevo mestizaje*, the rising hybrid reality." As early as his doctoral dissertation, "Mexico y su novela policial," he was invoking Mikhail Bakhtin's concept of hybridity to examine the mingling of high and low cultures in Mexican detective fiction. Stavans repeatedly presents intermingling as a cultural ideal, even, during an aside in *What Is La Hispanidad?* (Stavans and Jakšić 123), hinting at mixed marriage as a solution to social disorder. He does, though, acknowledge that even the category of "Hispanic" contains within itself disparate multitudes. "In my view," he says, "the effort at unifying such a multiheaded monster is daunting, so diverse and heterogeneous is the civilization at its core" (123).

The Melting Pot was for many decades the conventional model for achieving national unity and defining *la americanidad*. Each puts aside cultural idiosyncrasies and merges into a common identity. However, "melting" demands more of a sacrifice by some than others; an immigrant from Mexico or China must relinquish much more than one from England or Canada. Though he cherishes the possibility of a national conversation, Stavans insists that it be conducted in many voices, even many languages. So he is zealous about factoring Latinos, Jews, and other minorities into the equation and about finding a way to mix without melting. E pluribus unum is fine in principle, but daunting in practice. Much of Stavans's mission of engaging in haute vulgarisation is itself a juggling act between specialized expertise and generalizations accessible to the lay public. Is it possible for scholars to merge their abstruse insights into the common fund of knowledge? He counts himself an American because he relishes the opportunity to tame the multiheaded monster.

However, immediately after expressing his gratitude toward the United States, Stavans adds that he remains an alien: "But I don't believe it is the greatest country in the world. I don't even feel it is my country. Instead, it is simply where I live, my place of residence" (Stavans and Gracia 184). It would probably be impertinent to ask him which country he believes *is* the greatest country in the world, since he is skeptical, if not cynical, toward national allegiance in general. "Patriotism," he contends, "is the ideology of the wicked and insecure" (Sokol 52). Though the wicked and insecure might draw comfort from waving and wrapping themselves in the flag, Stavans does not. "To me a flag is just a piece of cloth" (*With All Thine Heart* 120), he says, rejecting the symbolic system out of which patriotism is constructed. So it is not just flags that he is loath to salute. "This position of mine is an expression of the disconnection I feel toward any national paraphernalia: a flag, an anthem, the concept of 'sacred soil,' etc. To me these ideas are impossible to justify" (Stavans and Gracia 141). It might have been hard to maintain that position from 1977 to 1978, when he served as a nonconscripted soldier in the Mexican Army. However, as a writer, Stavans later came to reject any national label. "The only true country a writer can claim," he claims, "is the language in which he writes" ("Is American Literature Parochial?"). Since Stavans writes in two languages, he holds passports in both English and Spanish. Scornful of American "exceptionalism," he notes that every nation flatters itself for being exceptional.

Denouncing Jewish intellectuals for insufficient patriotism toward the Soviet Union, Stalinists branded them "rootless cosmopolitans" (*bezrodnyi kosmopolity*). In the 1940s, the epithet could bring deadly consequences. A proud citizen of the world, Stavans accepts the label as a badge of honor. Striving for a delicate balance between the universal and the particular, he is not ashamed of his Jewishness, but he characterizes cosmopolitanism as an extension of it. "As a Jew," he explains, "I understand my fate as a border crosser" (Durán 149). Neither is he ashamed to call himself an intellectual, a species that he also links to cosmopolitanism: "I tend to see the role of the intellectual as that of a traveler to a distant land whose mandate is to offer a comprehensive report on what his eyes see" (Sokol 55).

W. H. Auden lived in Manhattan for most of the last thirty-four years of his life, but after becoming a naturalized citizen, the Anglo-American poet, a native of York, identified himself as a New Yorker, not an American. Stavans, too, is enamored of the city he studied, worked, and lived in during his first years out of Mexico. He extols the vibrancy and diversity of a metropolis whose population is more than 35 percent foreign-born and where more than half of the residents speak a language other than English at home ("New York City Population"). Even after settling in a small town in western Massachusetts, he continued to feel a special bond with New York City, the Hispanic and Jewish capital of the United States. Though he was

The Restless Ilan Stavans

already living in Amherst, he felt the terrorist attacks on the World Trade Center in New York as a personal trauma, explaining that "in my own case, 9/11 ratified my embrace of the United States as *mi hogar*, my home" (Sokol 52).

But most of the time, Stavans revels in the extravagance of maintaining several spiritual homes. "A writer's true country is language, not place," he contends. "And one might have many countries. I certainly do. Am I a traitor because I refuse to choose one? I couldn't care less" (Durán 148). Stavans clearly does care about how he is perceived, or he would not take great pains in book after book to explain his attitude toward extraterritoriality. Although spies are often adept at slipping across borders and switching languages, he insists that indifference toward boundaries—geographical or linguistic—should not be construed as betrayal. His departure from Mexico does not constitute treason toward *la patria*, the fatherland; it is not a kind of psychic patricide. Nor is his abandonment of his native Spanish, *la lengua materna*, a form of matricide. He recognizes that his restlessness puts him at odds with readers who cherish a stable, sedentary existence, but he celebrates his discordance as much as his unsettledness. Stavans, who fancies himself a Socratic gadfly, in fact elevates dissension from conventional wisdom into an ethical principle and connects it to geographical displacement. "My contrarianism is intimately linked to my experience as an immigrant" (*Most Imperfect Union* xii), he explains. A process of defamiliarization, migration tests the assumptions that a native takes for granted.

So where does all that leave Stavans's experience of and attitude toward displacement? A resident—indeed, homeowner—in Amherst, Massachusetts, for almost half his life, he is not exactly homeless. His possession of a U.S. passport signifies a certain closure to the process of immigration begun when he abandoned Mexico for New York in 1985. However, Stavans maintains dual citizenship, implying at least some ambivalence—and contrariness—toward the traditional paradigm of immigration. In *Reclaiming Travel*, he and coauthor Joshua Ellison invoke travel writer Bruce Chatwin's concept of "the nomadic alternative." They explain that "a nomad has the ability to be at home anywhere" (2). Clearly, neither Stavans nor Ellison nor most of their readers would ever be at home in the Amazon rainforest, the Mongolian steppe, or a bedroll under a highway overpass in Los Angeles. However, they posit the nomad as an aspirational icon, the embodiment of the virtues of malleability, agility, and adaptability.

Furthermore, with Stavans's dialectical mentality, they view mobility as a counterpoint to the sedentary life. The nomadic alternative is, after all, an alternative, and if transience were adopted as the exclusive norm, Stavans the proud contrarian would surely rebel against it as well. "Civilization and nomadism," they note, "far from being at odds, are really the twin impulses that make us human" (3). Each polarity, civilization and nomadism, can be understood only in terms of the other. And if each complements the other in order to make us fully human, we are all at best simultaneously indigenes and immigrants.

To more than sixty million contemporary refugees, the nomadic alternative might seem the idle fantasy of a privileged few. To those fleeing war, famine, poverty, crime, or natural disaster, borders are not abstractions but lethal obstacles. If, according to Robert Frost, "Home is the place where, when you have to go there, / They have to take you in" ("The Death of the Hired Man"), many today are homeless, drifting among nations that are loath to take them in. For them, national identity and language are not a matter of choice but circumstance. Adaptable by necessity more than philosophy, they practice a different kind of mobility.

7 LION PROWLING THE ACADEMY

> In the academic world, most of the work that is
> done is clerical. A lot of the work done by profes-
> sors is routine. . . . I have known people who are
> working class or craftsmen, who happen to be
> more intellectual than professors.
>
> —**Noam Chomsky (Solomon)**

Although he is one of the most famous professors in the United States and even identified himself as "writer/professor" on his passport, Stavans declares: "I have never fully made peace with myself as an academic" (*On Borrowed Words* 180). Waging war against academics, he in fact rarely passes up an opportunity to denounce the species to which he belongs. He faults them for being isolated and sedentary and admits that the very word *academic* "makes my skin crawl" (Sokol 62). Rather than the proverbial self-hating Jew, Stavans is another familiar figure: the self-loathing academic. In a conversation with another professor, Morris Dickstein, Stavans explains that "*academic* is a noun I feel uncomfortable with. In my mind academics are ostriches: they bury their head underground" (*Singer's Typewriter* 278). The contemporary academic institutions he observes—filled with careerists, partisans, and dullards—seem, at least in idealized hindsight, antithetical in spirit to the Athenian Academy that, inspired by the gadfly Socrates, cultivated genuinely free reflection. Part of Stavans's distaste for the word *academic* might derive from his loathing of Spain's Real Academia Española, an official institution that, acting to calcify the living Spanish language, has declared war on the Spanglish he loves.

Deploring "the intellectual stagnation that takes place in universities and colleges nationwide" (Sokol 153), Stavans contends that "the hardest thing for academics is to think for themselves" (Stavans and Jakšić 67). And, presenting a rather unflattering portrait of his colleagues as frauds and dolts, he reports: "I spend my days among academics in the humanities, a vast majority of whom make a profession of being pretentious" (*Critic's Journey* 116). Calling to mind Harold Rosenberg's scathing phrase "a herd of independent minds," he characterizes academics as timid conformists: "Academics are domesticated intellectuals: they are complacent in their tenured positions, dreaming of freedom of speech but rarely exercising it" (Sokol 58). Most academics are not, in fact, tenured. Their precarious position as assistant professors and adjuncts might highlight how the system enforces servility over intellectual independence.

It is hard to think of George Steiner, who has held prestigious academic positions at the University of Cambridge, Harvard University, the University of Oxford, and the University of Geneva, as just another institutional drudge. Cosmopolitan, polymath, and polyglot (fluent in English, French, and German), Steiner would seem to be the apotheosis of what Stavans looks for in a critic. Instead, in *The Oven*, a dramatic monologue he subtitles *An Anti-Lecture*, Steiner functions as the anti-Stavans. Stavans begins his autobiographical account of an entheogenic experience among the Putumayo people of the Colombian Amazon by attacking Steiner as "aloof, presumptuous, condescending." Rather than praise Steiner for his extraterritorial erudition, he states that "he is one of those I often read *against*, to find out not so much what he says but what I think about it" (*The Oven* 7). The critique of Steiner for his alleged arrogance and intellectual rigidity serves as the launching point for a three-day episode in which Stavans opens himself to the unknown by submitting humbly to a shaman who administers a dose of the psychotropic substance ayahuasca. In an account of the incident that he wrote for the *Chronicle of Higher Education*, Stavans describes how the experience liberated and loosened him, making him a better, because more flexible and open, teacher after he returned to Massachusetts: "Faced with rigidity, I improvise. I'm not afraid to make a fool of myself, although I'm careful not to be clownish. I want students to witness, along with me, the façade authority often becomes. My purpose is not only to invite them to feel vulnerable too, but to embrace vulnerability as strength" ("Professor's Journey"). Stavans is frequently asked about his attitude toward academics. And it seems as if his assessment becomes more hyperbolically negative with each of the dozens of interviews he gives. By 2012, he was telling Philip K. Jason: "For me the noun academic is derogatory: it denotes affectation, posturing, pretense. Academic life is shamefully aloof, removed from the nuts-and-bolts affairs of daily Americans. I feel uncomfortable with such elitism: I prefer to get my hands dirty, to delve into the frying pan" (Jason). Stick your hands into a frying pan—or a melting pot—and you are bound to be burned. The hostility that Stavans has aroused in Roberto González Echevarría, Louis Mendoza, Tey Diana Rebolledo, and others is a warning that when you denounce the culinary skills of full professors, the academy bites back. Taking "theorization" as the sine qua non of sanctioned academic publication, Mendoza accuses Stavans of producing "undertheorized scholarship" (Mendoza 84).

Elena Machado Sáez has taken perhaps the most mordant bite. Echoing others who challenge the authority of a middle-class migrant from Mexico City to speak for Latinos, she accuses Stavans of adopting a "Eurocentric colonialist" approach to their experience. He ignores, she claims, the economic and political forces that have shaped that experience. Stavans the logophile himself makes no secret of his privileging of language, but Sáez argues that his celebration of Spanish—and Spanglish—makes him complicit with conquistadors, leading him to erase indigenous cultures from his discussions. Some of Sáez's critique oddly resembles Stavans's own complaint about the Iberocentrism of his graduate school professors at Columbia.

She even faults Stavans for championing the work of Felipe Alfau. Stavans describes Alfau, who, after immigrating to the United States from Spain, became one of the first writers to switch from Spanish to English, as a foundational figure in Latino culture. But Sáez, who attacks "the conservative colonialist logic operating within the language-based definition of Latinidad used by Stavans" (Sáez 414), mocks the idea of nominating "a fascist Spaniard as founding father of U.S. Latino/a literature" (421). She finds Stavans guilty of sympathy for a supporter of right-wing tyranny. Sáez uses the example of Stavans as an argument for a radical reconfiguration of Latino/a Studies in the university beyond the scope of English and Spanish departments. Privileging economic and/or political forces over language would not necessarily yield a more comprehensive understanding, especially if the Wittgensteinian premise that the limits of language are the limits of mind is valid. Moreover, Sáez's discomfort with outsiders as observers would also force a radical reconstruction not only of English and Spanish departments but also of anthropology departments. The observer is always outside that which is observed.

Stavans's attitude toward intellectuals and academics in many ways echoes the analysis provided by Russell Jacoby in his 1987 polemic *The Last Intellectuals: American Culture in the Age of Academe*. Trying to understand what accounts for a "missing generation" of American intellectuals, Jacoby examines the careers of such 1950s thinkers as Michael Harrington, Jane Jacobs, Alfred Kazin, C. Wright Mills, Lewis Mumford, and Edmund Wilson. He names Stanley Aronowitz, Marshall Berman, and Richard Sennett (but not Ilan Stavans, who had not yet published his first book) as possible successors, but he deplores the general paucity of contemporary thinkers who communicate clearly to the general educated public. Jacoby blames suburbanization, the demise of an urban bohemia, and academic careerism for writing that is overly specialized and inaccessible to all but a few fellow initiates. What he calls the "Age of Academe" is the windmill against which Stavans is tilting his lance.

As with both the Latino and Jewish communities, Stavans is thus both an outsider and an insider to the kind of academic life that most experience throughout the United States. Unlike the research factories of the large state and private universities, Amherst College has fewer than two thousand students. It is an exclusive and exclusively undergraduate institution that, through light teaching loads and small classes, encourages close interaction between instructors and students. Stavans does not supervise graduate students training to become professors. The undergraduates in his seminars are more likely bound for careers in medicine, law, or business than in academe as scholars of literature. Instead, as in his writing, Stavans the teacher can and must be an engaging generalist, an endearingly vulpine polymath, not the pedantic hedgehog who is his prototypical academic. He faults fellow academics, "whose blah-blah-blah is noisy but meaningless and whose approach to a book is defined not by passion but mechanism" (*Inveterate Dreamer* xi), for being overly specialized and impenetrably opaque. "Writing for them," he complains, "is about obfuscation: rather than enlightening a discussion, they make it more obscure" (*Critic's Journey* 116). Such drones, according to Stavans, can be counted on to produce "the academic essay, obtuse in content, obscure in language, meant for a minuscule audience of five colleagues" (31). He constructs his straw man out of the leaves of unreadable and unread professional journals.

In contrast to academics who embed esoteric jargon in convoluted sentences accessible only to initiates, Stavans proclaims "simplicity, clarity, and straightforwardness" as his guiding principles. Rejecting Jacques Derrida's valorization of difficulty, he affirms his elective affinities with Confucius, who observed that "life is really simple but we insist on making it complicated." Obfuscation is, therefore, distortion and dishonesty. Stavans also echoes Albert Einstein's belief that "if you can't explain a difficult idea to a six-year-old, you yourself don't understand it" ("Friday Takeaway: On Aging"). It was possible to explain counterpoint to six-year-old Mozart, but Gayatri Spivak would have a difficult time making her postcolonial poststructuralist circumlocutions comprehensible to a child. For that matter, though, it is doubtful that Einstein could explain the special theory of relativity to a tot.

Though Euclides da Cunha was elected to the Academia Brasileira de Letras, following publication of his masterpiece *Os Sertões* (*Backlands: The Canudos Campaign*) in 1902, he was not an academic, but a journalist. In an Introduction he wrote to da Cunha's sophisticated account of the Brazilian government's military action against a rebellious Bahia town, Stavans confers one of his favorite titles on the author: "polymath" (Introduction to *Backlands* xi). Admiring da Cunha's "encyclopedic knowledge" (xvii), he contends that "he exemplifies the modern thinker who wanders and wonders at the same time" (xvii). Those are precisely the open and fluid qualities that Stavans himself aspires to and that he finds lacking in contemporary academics.

Unlike conventional scholarly prose, his essays are unabashedly personal and subjective. It would be considered uncouth to include analysis of the scholar's own dreams in an article published in *Modern Philology* or *Papers on Language and Liter-*

ature, but not only does Stavans make routine use of the forbidden first-person pronoun, he often grounds a discussion in a dream he had. Typical is the way he opens *Resurrecting Hebrew*, recounting a nocturnal vision he had of a beautiful woman who spoke Hebrew that was incomprehensible to him. Memoirs are supposed to be personal, but one critic, Thane Rosenbaum, who is both a novelist and an academic, faulted *On Borrowed Words* for being *too* personal, insisting that "his book would have been more affective had he concentrated less on the personal and more on the translated knowledge he has acquired from the lands he has traveled and books he has read" (Rosenbaum). Before completing his doctorate at Columbia, Stavans was, like da Cunha, a journalist, contributing to newspapers such as the *Forward* and the *New York Times Book Review*—in English—and *Excélsior, Diario 16, El Nacional*, and *El Diario/La Prensa*—in Spanish.

However, as a professor, he almost never writes for scholarly journals, the kinds of publications that require abstracts and endnotes and subject submissions to peer review, though it is clear that he draws on such scholarship in his own more accessible essays and talks. His 2010 study of the early years of Gabriel García Márquez is one of the few Stavans volumes with endnotes, bibliography, and index. Stavans repeatedly holds up Edmund Wilson, the influential American literary and cultural critic who died in 1972, as his professional model and tutelary spirit. Others in his personal pantheon include Isaiah Berlin, Irving Howe, Samuel Johnson, Franz Kafka, Octavio Paz, Don Quixote, Sholem Aleichem, and Baruch Spinoza. It is surprising that Stavans has written only briefly about Susan Sontag, an outspoken Jewish intellectual who, operating outside academe, wrote lucidly, without footnotes. He patronizes her as "the matron saint of chic resistance" (*Critic's Journey* 161).

A scourge of professional pedants, Wilson wrote for the *New Republic*, the *New Yorker*, the *New York Review of Books*, and *Vanity Fair*, but never for *PMLA* or *Philological Quarterly*. After earning a BA from Princeton, he never pursued an advanced degree, and, except for a year, 1964–65, as a fellow of the Center for Advanced Studies at Wesleyan University, was unaffiliated with any academic institution. However, he was a voraciously inquisitive autodidact who made himself knowledgeable enough to write credibly about the Dead Sea Scrolls, the Civil War, and the Russian Revolution, in addition to the canon of modern literature. "In short," Stavans contends, "Wilson is a paradigm: he's the ultimate generalist: he didn't write about anything but about everything. Plus, his essays are always [a] pleasure to read, which is more than one might say about scores of authors, especially in academia" (Sokol 72).

It should be noted that Stavans holds up Wilson—"a consummate dilettante with an enviable critical eye" (*Critic's Journey* 118)—as a paragon against whom to shame not only academics but also contemporary critics. Noting that "what passes for reflection on books and literary themes is generally of embarrassing quality," he offers a baleful diagnosis of the condition of commentary: "Literary criticism is in deep trouble in the United States today" (*Critic's Journey* 116). However, Stavans's attack on fellow critics is not nearly as scathing or obsessive as his attack on fellow academics.

Though Stavans is comfortably moored at an academic address, he delights in razzing academics. Some return his disdain in kind. Roberto González Echevarría, the Sterling Professor of Hispanic and Comparative Literature at Yale (and perhaps a model for the pedantic renegade from New Haven who taunts Stavans in *El Iluminado*), has been a particularly avid scourge of Stavans's lapses in scholarly rigor. Reviewing Stavans's edition of *Rubén Darío: Selected Writings*, which he derided as a "carelessly conceived and executed anthology," González Echevarría offered a devastating inventory of the volume's flaws:

> Stavans's introduction lacks scholarly credibility or academic reliability. It is riddled with clichés (Darío is a "man for all seasons"), lacks a single new idea worth considering and does no justice to the considerable body of Darío criticism. Like the translations, it contains elementary mistakes, some laughable. For instance, Stavans attributes the famous line encouraging poets to reject Darío by twisting the swan's neck to the Mexican Modernista Manuel Gutiérrez Nájera, when it was written by his compatriot Enrique González Martínez. He also blithely declares that "Latin America never had a Romantic movement per se," an elementary error that he could have avoided by reading any history of Latin American literature or one of those academic critics Stavans derides with unearned, comic self-assurance. Stavans even writes that Darío's "health deteriorated rapidly in the years following World War I," when the poet had been dead for two years at war's end in 1918. His health could hardly have gotten worse. (González Echevarría, "Master of Modernismo")

A careful, less flamboyant, less productive academic might not have made himself as vulnerable to evisceration by a prominent professor.

Nevertheless, it is clear that Stavans aspires to be the Jewish Latino Edmund Wilson. Though he might admire the multilingualism of the critic who studied Greek, Latin, French, Italian, German, Russian, Hebrew, and Hungarian, he would be disappointed by Wilson's aversion to Spanish. And he might cringe at Wilson's pronouncements about Hispanic culture and its literary crown jewel, *Don Quixote*. "I have been bored by Hispanophiles," Wilson wrote in the *New Yorker* in 1965, "and I have also been bored by everything, with the exception of Spanish painting, that I have ever known about Spain. I have made a point of learning no Spanish, and I have never got through 'Don Quixote'" (*Edmund Wilson Celebration* 81). Stavans's output already exceeds that of his hero, Wilson. Part of that output is the three-volume set of the writings of Isaac Bashevis Singer that Stavans edited. Impressed by what the *Bibliothèque de la Pléiade* did in producing a definitive library of canonical French literature, Wilson had called for the creation of a set of comprehensive, inexpensive editions of the classics of American literature.

In two essays that appeared in successive issues of the *New York Review of Books* in 1968, Wilson railed against the Modern Language Association's practice of recovering trivial and discarded texts by literary masters and including them in costly "definitive editions." This literary refuse might be of use to specialists he argued: "But beyond this, for the ordinary reader, who is not obliged to use them for a Ph.D. thesis, these papers have no interest whatever" (Wilson, "Fruits of the MLA: II"). Stavans shares Wilson's disdain for the MLA and for lifeless, joyless, specialized scholarship. His own role in publishing such obscure writers as Alicia Freilich, Efraín Huerta, Teresa Porzecanski, and Mauricio Rosencof might strike Wilson as overly specialized. But in his own editing work, Stavans, too, has endeavored to make major writers—Rubén Darío, Pablo Neruda, César Vallejo—accessible and pleasurable to general readers. That has also been the goal of The Library of America, which was created ten years after Wilson's death in 1972 as a fulfillment of his dream of an American Pléiade. It is fitting that, in 2004, it was Stavans who brought Isaac Bashevis Singer into The Library of America, by editing for it a three-volume edition of Singer's *Collected Stories* as well as *Isaac Bashevis Singer: An Album*, an illustrated survey of Singer's life and work.

Stavans's emulation of Wilson is apparent not only in his pride in being a generalist polymath but also in his style. For the epigraph to his lexicographical meditations, *Dictionary Days* (2005), he appropriates a sentence from Ludwig Wittgenstein's *Tractatus Logico-Philosophicus*: "What can be said at all can be said clearly" (*Dictionary Days*). In the historical dialectic between plain and precious, Francisco de Quevedo and Luis de Góngora, Ernest Hemingway and William Faulkner, George Orwell and Jacques Derrida, Stavans, obeying *lex parsimoniae*, comes down on the side of simplicity and lucidity. One of the reasons that he admires Edmund Wilson is that "Wilson's prose is a model of clarity and conviction" (Sokol 61).

Stavans's enduring fascination with the work of Jorge Luis Borges, another champion of the lucid style, is evident in *Borges, the Jew* (2016), a book-length reflection on the Argentine's "relentless desire (not to be confused with envy) to claim, as part of his self, a Jewishness he found in books, in idols such as Baruch Spinoza, in an overall attitude, at once reverential and subversive, toward God, life, and the intellect" (*Borges* ix–x). Stavans's elective affinity with Borges manifests itself in the conceptual playfulness of his own short fiction; "Xerox Man," for example, a story, published in the collection *The Disappearance* (2006), about an Orthodox thief who steals rare books in order to photocopy them, is a Borgesian meditation on originality. The novella *Talia in Heaven* borrows mirrors, labyrinths, and even an aleph from the Argentine master. One reviewer noted that the "cribbings of signature motifs from Borges . . . seems compulsive" (Christophersen). Stavans confesses that, at an early stage in his career: "My only hope as a litterateur was not to be like Borges, but to *be* Borges" (*On Borrowed Words* 8). However, in order to overcome this anxiety of influence, to find his own voice, Stavans recounts the day he took all the volumes by Borges that he owned and, in "a sacramental act of desperation: the struggle to be born, to own a place of my own, to be like no one else—or at least, unlike Borges" (*On Borrowed Words 9*), he set fire to them all.

However, accepting his own status as a Xerox man, Stavans appears not to suffer from Harold Bloom's anxiety of influence. "I am a copy, an instant replay, a shadow, an imposter," he declares. "Everything is an echo. To live is to plagiarize, to imitate, to steal" (*Inveterate Dreamer* 262). If there is no such thing as originality, then why not produce fiction that is pastiche? Or pastiche of pastiche? Stavans imitates Borges, the master appropriator who, most notably in "Pierre Menard, autor del Quijote," ponders the case of a twentieth-century Frenchman who "translates" Cervantes's novel by reproducing its seventeenth-century Spanish sentences verbatim. "A Land Without Crows" is an imaginary letter from Franz Kafka to his friend Max Brod. In "The One-Handed Pianist," in which a pianist named Malvina suddenly discovers that her left hand has abandoned her, Stavans imitates Nikolai Gogol's story "The Nose," in which Major Kovalyov is abruptly left without his proboscis. In his nonfiction as in his metafiction, Stavans impresses not by saying things never said before as much as by the range and aptness of what he says.

Borges, like Wilson, exerts his influence over Stavans most powerfully in his style: "His pure, precise, almost mathematical style; his intelligent plots; his abhorrence of verborrea—the overflow of words without end of reason, still a common malady in Spanish literature today" (*On Borrowed Words* 7). Shaving with Ockham's Razor, Stavans writes his adopted English in the manner prescribed by H. W. Fowler and F. G. Fowler in the legendary guidebook they called *The King's English*: "Any one who wishes to become a good writer should endeavour, before he allows himself to be tempted by the more showy qualities, to be direct, simple, brief, vigorous, and lucid" (1).

One factor influencing Stavans's style is the fact that he does most of his writing in English, a language that does not flow naturally and untrammeled from his pen. When Samuel Beckett switched from English to French, his playful, digressive style became terse and austere. Asked why he would deliberately handicap himself by forsaking the copiousness of his native tongue for an adopted language in which he could not hope to be nearly as virtuosic, Beckett replied, "parce qu'en français, c'est plus facile d'écrire sans style" (Gessner 32n) (because in French, it's easier to write without style). Of course, writing without style, whatever that might mean, is an unattainable ideal; even what Roland Barthes characterizes as *Le Degré zéro de l'écriture* (the zero degree of writing) in the spare sentences of Albert Camus *is* a style

(Barthes). Vladimir Nabokov, who also switched languages, faulted Beckett's translingual texts: "Beckett's French is a schoolmaster's French, a preserved French, but in English you feel the moisture of verbal association and of the spreading live roots of his prose" (Nabokov 172). The plain style might seem the default strategy of writers who acquire their language through textbooks rather than their mothers' lullabies. In his play *La Cantatrice chauve* (1950), Eugène Ionesco uses simplistic French, not his native Romanian, to mock his own attempts to learn English by repeating inane phrases from a language primer. However, Nabokov's own lavish lexicon and Joseph Conrad's tortuous syntax contradict any claim that literary translinguals must necessarily follow Fowler.

The principal reason that Stavans avoids recondite vocabulary and convoluted sentences is that he is writing for the general educated reader, not specialists. In her review of his book on José Vasconcelos, Andrea Pagni suggests that Stavans's implied reader is more likely to be familiar with Stavans's writing than the Mexican philosopher's: "Se trata, por lo tanto, de que esa comunidad de lectores para la que Stavans publica este libro, su lector implícito y en parte explícito, que cita a Vasconcelos sin haberlo leído, conozca sus escritos, leyéndolos de la mano de quien ofrece una perspectiva crítica y a la vez abierta" (Pagni 247). An introduction to the Bible is quite different from a commentary written for Talmudic colleagues. And because scholars read other scholars out of duty, not pleasure, there is little need to entice them. Because they are already quite familiar with the topic, it is possible, even necessary, to employ jargon that might seem foreign to lay readers. Based on his doctoral dissertation, *Antiheroes: Mexico and Its Detective Novel* is probably Stavans's most traditional work of scholarship. But even it was hailed—in the pages of the otherwise prim *Modern Language Review* and even in translation—as "a cracking good read" (Swanson 1143).

Unable to take his readers for granted, Stavans must seduce them with the power of his words. Note the brevity, even bluntness, of the opening sentences in Stavans's books:

"I am packing my library" (*On Borrowed Words*).

"'Do words die?' asked my eight-year-old Isaiah one afternoon" (*Dictionary Days*).

"I had a pleasant dream in which I saw the future in our Americas" (*The Hispanic Condition*).

"Throughout his life, Borges was overwhelmed by a strange feeling of unworthiness" (*Borges, the Jew*).

"Excess" (*Bandido*).

Stavans inserts hooks to coax a reader to turn his pages. To sober scholars, that might seem like lurid murals in a Calvinist church. Put off by his breezy conversational tone, some might resent his glibness. Surely complex thoughts require complex sentences, devotees of Hegel assume, not the single bare subject-predicate of much of Stavans's prose.

The opening sentence of *Octavio Paz: A Meditation* (2001) states: "There is no sense in pursuing a literary career under the impression that one is operating a bombing-plane, Edmund Wilson once said" (3). A responsible scholar immediately wonders: When did Wilson say that? Where? Why are there no quotation marks around Wilson's alleged statement? However, nowhere in the entire book does Stavans cite a source for that or any other assertion (Wilson, in fact, made the remark in a 1937 essay called "American Critics, Left and Right"; a sober scholar could point out that it can be found on page 595 of *The Edmund Wilson Reader*, ed. Lewis M. Dabney, New York: Da Capo Press, 1997). Stavans provides *Octavio Paz* with the subtitle *A Meditation* and gives *Reflections on Jewish Culture* as the subtitle of *Singer's Typewriter and Mine* and *Reflections on Culture and Identity in America* as the subtitle of *The Hispanic Condition*. He characterizes *Bandido* as "a biographical investigation" (*Bandido* 12). Meditations, reflections, and investigations are continuing processes, not the finished products of sedulous research.

They also emphasize the subjectivity of the author. Stavans's slim book on Octavio Paz is an unapologetically personal discussion by a self-described "devotee and incessant reader" (*Octavio Paz* 4). Though it concedes that "nothing even remotely [resembling?] a friendship existed between us" (4), it begins by noting that he met Paz twice and spoke to him by phone once. Stavans begins his biographical study of Gabriel García Márquez from birth through the publication of *One Hundred Years of Solitude* by recalling the rainy April afternoon in Mexico City in 1982 when he discovered and devoured the novel that had been published fifteen years before. *Gabriel García Márquez: The Early Years* concludes with a statement about its author, not its subject. "I was wrong, of course," Stavans admits (182), about his expectation that García Márquez's literary career would end with the triumph of *One Hundred Years of Solitude*. Similarly, in *Bandido*, Stavans is intent on examining his own impressions of Acosta, whom he imagines as his doppelgänger, "partly myself and vice versa" (*Bandido* 12). He is more interested in using Acosta, whom he never met, as a pretext for thinking about contemporary culture—"He personifies the alienation, disdain, insecurity, oppression, the whole love-hate relationship of Chicanos to America" (*Bandido* 124)—than in arriving at an "objective" account of his life, even if that were possible. Like Acosta himself as well as other contemporaries such as Norman Mailer, Hunter S. Thompson, and Tom Wolfe, Stavans is writing the kind of New Journalism that abjures the pretense of neutrality and places the writer in the middle of the story.

Though Stavans denounces as arcane gibberish much of what passes for academic publication, most academics in the humanities devote at least as much of their time to teaching as to research. Many professors are no doubt dedicated, inspired, and inspiring teachers, and, without access to other classrooms, Stavans is understandably wary of issuing a blanket condemnation of literary pedagogy in American higher education, other than to conclude his modest audit by asserting: "My impression is that literary studies are bankrupt" (*Critic's Journey* 191). Bankruptcy courts usually require more detailed documentation. However, his characterization of departments of Spanish, populated, he claims, by "ostriches" who divide themselves into insular camps of *peninsularistas* and *latinoamericanistas*, is particularly scathing. They are, he complains, "imprisoned in a premodern mentality, misanthropic in nature, alienated, reacting rather than acting" ("Against the Ostrich Syndrome" 61).

Stavans recalls his own experience as a graduate student as "an unhappy one" (*Critic's Journey* 190) and portrays the graduate school at Columbia University as an elitist "ivory tower" (*On Borrowed Words* 237). In particular, the Department of Spanish, in which he enrolled, was, by his account, an anachronistic conservator of canonized—and fossilized—Iberian culture: "It applauded masters like Cervantes, Lope de Vega, and Góngora without establishing connections between their time and ours; and the teachers' views of Latin America and the Caribbean were of a wasteland where only exorcism and magic dared to emerge. The bridge between the public and the academic spheres was fragile at best" (*On Borrowed Words* 238). One venerable professor, Félix Martínez-Bonati (whose name Stavans misspells as Bonatti), cautioned his industrious graduate student against publishing too frequently in dailies and monthlies, which he dismissed as unworthy of his time and talent. According to Martínez-Bonati, the true scholar does not write on demand. "His only deadline is the grave" (*On Borrowed Words* 238). Stavans lacks the patience of his academic advisers.

Nevertheless, Stavans was not deterred from writing for lay readers or from serving as a bridge between the public and academic spheres. As the topic for his dissertation at Columbia, he chose a popular genre then considered beneath the dignity of serious scholars. And Alfred J. MacAdam, the longtime editor of the biannual *Review: Latin-American Literature and Arts*, an intellectual but nonscholarly magazine that was perhaps an inspiration for *Hopscotch: A Cultural Review*—which Stavans founded in 1999 and edited until its demise in 2001—agreed to supervise it. Signed with his birth name, Ilán Stavchansky, "Mexico y su novela policial" (Mexico and Its Detective Novel) begins with an argument for the value of studying noncanonical work. However, unlike anything he would ever write again, the dissertation, successfully defended in 1990, includes twelve pages of endnotes. It also deals with such genre writers as Antonio Helu, Jorge Ibarguengoitia, Vicente Lenero, and Rodolfo Usigli, whom Stavans would rarely if ever return to. He would, though, sustain his enthusiasm for popular culture, declaring in the title of an essay: "¡Viva el Kitsch!" (*Essential Ilan Stavans* 147–49). In the same essay, he confesses his youthful love for burritos at Taco Bell and says that "comic strips and cartoons were my favorite pastime" (170).

By 1990, Stavans's interests did not exactly brand him as a lone wolf in higher education. The Popular Culture Association, reacting against what its founders, Ray Browne and Russell Nye, perceived as the narrowness of academe's literary canon, held its first conference in 1971. Dedicated to the study of books, music, movies, comics, and other manifestations of material culture traditionally spurned by credentialed scholars, the Popular Culture movement spread rapidly, with its own journals, books, and conferences. Emphasizing his personal rebellion against the same forces that Stavans, too, found stifling, Browne titled his history of the movement *Against Academia* (1989). While Stavans was writing his dissertation on Mexican detective novels, the Popular Culture Association had already become an academic empire of its own, with half a dozen regional affiliates, international activities, and annual conferences that drew two thousand participants. Browne had even begun designing a PhD in Popular Culture at Bowling Green State University. In the final decade of the twentieth century, it was not entirely unprecedented or foolhardy for an academic to be against academia.

However, unlike most other academics, Stavans has, from the earliest stages of his career, targeted his essays and books at nonspecialists. From the privileged position of an endowed chair at Amherst College, Stavans constructs the bridge between public and academic spheres that he missed at Columbia. By most accounts, he is an imaginative and effective teacher, both at Amherst and at the many other institutions, including Bennington, Columbia, Doshisha (Japan), Oberlin, Stanford-Chile, Universidad Diego Portales, and the University of Texas at San Antonio, where he has been a visiting lecturer. In spring 2016, he even taught Shakespeare to a group of inmates at the Hampshire County Jail in Northampton, Massachusetts. Moreover, in 2003, he became one of three cofounders of the Great Books Summer Program, a literary summer camp in which middle and high school students spend eight weeks on the campus of Amherst, Stanford, Oxford, or Trinity College Dublin studying masters such as Jorge Luis Borges, Emily Dickinson, Homer, Seneca, and William Shakespeare. As both a teacher and a critic, Stavans challenges archaic models of what it is to be an *academic*, though it should be noted that the authors he teaches in the "Great Books" program represent the same supposedly calcified canon that he otherwise rejects as symptomatic of the paralysis of academics. At the same time, though, he has been moving more and more away from texts of dense print in favor of visual forms—evident not only in his *I Love My Selfie* (2017) but also in the fotonovela *Once@9:53am* (Stavans and Brodsky 2016), the children's picture book *Golemito* (2013), and the several comics—*Latino USA* (2000), *Mr. Spic Goes to*

Washington (2008), *El Iluminado* (Stavans and Sheinkin 2012), *A Most Imperfect Union* (2014), *Angelitos* (2018)—he has published.

As he aged and as the general culture grew more indifferent and even hostile toward book-learning, Stavans seemed to mellow. By 2017, he was promoting the "classics" that, as the incendiary graduate student who spurned Spanish Golden Age texts, he might have rejected as inert. "I love books," he was now proclaiming. "My mission is to make students love them as well. I open them in front of their eyes. Not just any book, but what I call 'tested books' by writers of all backgrounds—Plato, Shakespeare, Emily Dickinson, Dostoyevsky, James Baldwin, Grace Paley, Gabriel García Márquez—that have survived the passing of time. In other words, the classics" ("Friday Takeaway: Teaching"). And he was issuing a passionate defense of the teaching profession: "The classroom is where intellectual curiosity is at home, where our cultural values are shaped. It is where people think, individually as well as in group. For that reason, it is crucial that we again make teaching the revered, humble vocation it used to be" ("Friday Takeaway: Teaching"). While he might succeed in restoring some reverence in the profession, it will surely not be as a humble savant.

In order to understand Stavans's personal project as teacher and critic, it is necessary to parse his distinction between *academic* and *intellectual*—in fact, *public intellectual*, though the phrase is redundant since intellectuals are by definition public. Current usage of the English word *intellectual* derives from the French *intellectuel*, employed in the final years of the nineteenth century to designate Anatole France, Octave Mirbeau, Emile Zola, and other writers who deployed the power of their pens to fight the anti-Semitism that had sent Captain Alfred Dreyfus to Devil's Island on spurious charges of treason. The Dreyfusards were not merely thinkers; convinced of their social responsibility, they were transmitting and applying their thoughts to the public sphere in order to effect change. They identified a flagrant injustice and determined that it was their responsibility to use their talents to combat it. Zola's death under suspicious circumstances in 1902 suggests that the author of "J'accuse" might have been a martyr to the cause of writing the truth.

As a judge on the United States Court of Appeals Seventh Circuit, a lecturer at the University of Chicago Law School, and a prolific writer on matters of public concern, Richard A. Posner has been a controversial contemporary specimen of the intellectual. In *Public Intellectuals: A Study of Decline*, Posner offers this working definition of the species: "The intellectual writes for the general public, or at least for a broader than merely academic or specialist audience, on 'public affairs'—on *political* matters in the broadest sense of that word, a sense that includes cultural matters when they are viewed under the aspect of ideology, ethics, or politics (which may all be the same thing)" (23). Posner is convinced that intellectuals are in decline because American universities, fragmented into disciplines, encourage specialization and discourage attempts to address readers outside the academy or even outside an author's narrow specialty. Stavans does not share Posner's conservative ideology, but he, too, deplores the compartmentalization of thought in American research factories (i.e., universities) and the failure of thinkers to speak cogently to the educated public. Complaining to an interviewer about the sterile pedantry of academic life, Stavans contended that "unfortunately, criticism has been kidnapped by the academy, which has overwhelmed with rubbish. The academic essay—e.g., the tenure-track essay—is written for an audience of three or four lonely readers—for whom literature long ago ceased to be about pleasure—in order to become part of a profession. Yes, the worse [sic] that might happen to literature is institutionalization. For literature is free: free to make up things, free to associate, free to rebel" (Kameli). Caught up in a system that offers them the choice of publish or perish, academics churn out perishable prose.

In *A Critic's Journey*, Stavans recounts how, not long after his arrival in New York, his discovery of the Jewish newspaper the *Forward* helped inspire him in his calling as an intellectual. Founded in 1897 as the *Forverts*, it began as a Yiddish daily dedicated to the principles of democratic socialism and trade unionism and to covering topics of Jewish interest for a Jewish readership. By the early 1930s, it had become a major metropolitan daily, with a circulation of 275,000 and talented contributors who included Abraham Cahan, Leon Trotsky, and Isaac Bashevis Singer. By the time Stavans began reading the *Forward*, in the 1980s, its circulation had dwindled, and it was being published only once a week, with an English supplement that in 1990 became an independent publication whose circulation exceeded the Yiddish edition's. The English edition, to which Stavans would contribute, eventually became a monthly magazine and an online daily.

Faithful to the founding principles of the *Forward*, Stavans adopted this as his critic's credo: "I convinced myself that the only responsibility a writer has is to make full use of his talent as witness and participant of the time into which he was accidentally placed, to discern the major issues that define it, to use the imagination as mirror to better understand our place in history" (*Critic's Journey* 74). Note, again, the role of *accident* in Stavans's conception of the trajectory of his life, as well as, of course, his conception of the writer's responsibility to be witness and participant. He is noticeably silent about Paul de Man, Jacques Derrida, Gayatri Spivak, and other practitioners of theoretical abstractions that, he might contend, divert us from an understanding of our place in history. And while acknowledging, in passing, the aesthetic achievements of the high modernists, Stavans, championing the role of the writer as witness and participant, is wary of the elevation of their art of alienation into an end in itself. While his description of Marcel Proust's fictional masterpiece *A la recherche du temps perdu* as "an example of a self-serving, narcissistic genre . . . indulgent, hyperpsychological, and individualistic to a fault" (*Gabriel García Márquez*

97) echoes García Márquez, Stavans seems to endorse the verdict. Similarly, the claim that *"Finnegans Wake* was about nothing; it was about itself" (*Gabriel García Márquez* 98) appears to reflect Stavans's own distaste for what he might consider James Joyce's failure to bear the full responsibilities of a writer in his time. Unlike William Butler Yeats, Joyce never served in the Senate of the Irish Free State.

Despite his disappointment in the way that, in his view, the eminent Mexican critic Octavio Paz eventually rigidified into a political sellout and cultural despot, Paz is the Latin American intellectual Stavans admires most. "I emulate him vigorously" (*Octavio Paz* 82–83), he declares, somewhat awkwardly. Elsewhere, he calls Paz "a Renaissance man whom I admire wholeheartedly," though he expresses dismay that nowhere in all of Paz's writings is there "any serious consideration of Jewishness. So ubiquitous in Western Civilization, Jews seem to have been nonexistent in Paz's eyes" (*Critic's Journey* 67). The very first paragraph of Stavans's brief book-length reflections on Paz, which are in effect a meditation on what it is to be an intellectual, announces that "the duty of the intellectual is to serve as a compass, a road map" (*Octavio Paz* 3). In the example of Paz, as in his later book *Reclaiming Travel* (Stavans and Ellison), Stavans makes a virtue of movement, hence the imagery of compasses and maps. Paz, whose diplomatic service included postings in New York, Paris, Tokyo, Geneva, and Delhi, traveled widely out of professional duty and personal temperament. However, Stavans, seeing movement metaphorically, presents Paz as the quintessential figure of "the intellectual as ceaseless wayfarer" (*Octavio Paz* 39), whose wanderings are spiritual as much as geographical. He faults Paz for a conservative swerve in the final phase of his career, and he states that "his closeness to the status quo, his relentless need to be worshiped and applauded, his arrogant, imperious manners, and his depiction of European civilization as the ticket to Latin America's improvement" (*Art & Anger* 111) diminish the Nobel laureate's continuing influence. However, he credits Paz for influencing his own personal, restless literary style: "It was through reading his essays that I learned the pleasures and challenges of developing one's own ideas in rigorous, consistent yet jazzy and personal ways, that ideas never exist in isolation but in constant motion, coexisting with other ideas at all times, and that the free exchange of those ideas is an indispensable component in a free, healthy, and democratic society" (Introduction to *Monkey Grammarian*).

In his book about Paz, Stavans establishes the criteria by which he judges the Mexican author—and himself—as an intellectual. Contrasting his own views—"not as radical" (9)—with those of Noam Chomsky, he seems to mistake Chomsky's bitter critique of what Julien Benda called *la trahison des clercs* for an endorsement of the way American intellectuals have become "manufacturers of consent," pacifying tools of the reigning powers. "I also see the intellectual as an enlightened mind capable of exploring the nature and place of ideas," Stavans says. "But unlike Chomsky, I do not believe intellectuals have a duty to any power other than themselves" (9).

Chomsky certainly does not believe that intellectuals have a duty to serve the power of political or corporate rulers. Nevertheless, regardless of his misreading of Chomsky, what Stavans goes on to say is important for an understanding of his conception of the intellectual: "To survey the territory, the intellectual must take risks, wander about and around with eyes wide open, venture into unforeseen lands, make connections, make use of any tools at his disposal, and not take anything for granted in order to seize the meaning of his environment in full scope" (9). This view of the intellectual as constitutionally antithetical to complacency is consistent with Stavans's persistent valorization of restlessness and movement. When a thinker stops searching out new territory, she ceases to be an intellectual.

As the author of more than forty books and four hundred articles in English or Spanish and a pioneer in publicizing both the Latin American Boom and Chicano writing, Luis Leal, who was born in Mexico in 1907 and died in 2010, might seem Stavans's older alter ego. In fact, at the beginning of *A Luis Leal Reader*, which he edited in 2007, Stavans recalls, "I ended up becoming Leal for a couple of hours" (*Luis Leal Reader* ix). In 2003, he arranged to meet Leal for the first time in the restaurant of a hotel in New York City where the annual convention of the Modern Language Association was taking place. The MLA, an organization of about 25,000 teachers and scholars of languages and literatures, represents many of the academic qualities that make Stavans squirm. "I am not prone to visit such professional gatherings, which in my view resemble a flock of peacocks," he states. "I have made it my code of honor to avoid them as best as possible" (*Luis Leal Reader* vii). Apparently, ostriches evolve into peacocks when on public display. Despite his distaste for the MLA, however, Stavans decided that, since he was already there to meet Leal, he thought he might as well also stop by and see a friend at the conference. But, not a member of the MLA and lacking the necessary registration badge, Stavans was unable to pass through security to get inside the convention. So he borrowed Leal's badge, and for a few hours passed as one of the august senior authorities in Spanish studies.

While expressing admiration for Leal's scholarly achievements, Stavans also makes clear his misgivings about the venerable professor's limitations. After receiving his doctorate from the University of Chicago, Leal served on the faculty of several institutions, including the University of California at Santa Barbara, where he taught for more than thirty years. Unlike Stavans, who worked for a while as a newspaper correspondent after he came to the United States, Leal entered college immediately after immigrating, which, Stavans contends, means that "consequently, his worldview is less alien and confrontational, more sedate" (*Luis Leal Reader* ix). The adjective "sedate" reinforces Stavans's view that academe suppresses intellectual ferment, that, far from being a cultural stimulus, it is a sedative. During a conversation in which Leal points out how Latin American dictators stifled dissent through murder, torture, and exile, Stavans suggests to Leal that "the comfort of academia has a similar effect: it eradicates disagreement" (x). Despotic regimes enforced conformity and silence, whereas American universities encouraged smugness and mediocrity. Equating the two is hyperbolic, but it does demonstrate Stavans's strong antipathy to academic systems.

One might question how comfortable academia really is in institutions less insulated than wealthy Amherst College—whose endowment exceeds $2 billion and whose carefully selected students (if not receiving financial aid) pay more than $65,000 a year in tuition, room, and board—is from widespread social and economic problems. It is certainly not comfortable for the army of adjuncts—members of the precariat—who have been hired at mingy salaries, without job security, to teach a sizable percentage of undergraduates at big public universities. Those instructors have scant time and energy to produce the academic prose Stavans detests. Even for tenure-track instructors, it is a challenge to teach large classes of unprepared and unmotivated students. Disagreement has hardly been eradicated from academic committees that squabble over hiring, promotion, curriculum, and much else. The suggestion that dissent is as stifled in American universities as it was in Pinochet's Chile or in Argentina under the military junta is not only imprecise; it is specious. American universities have been cauldrons of protest against the war in Iraq, police shootings of black men, tuition hikes, the naming of campus buildings after contemptible people, sexual misconduct, the Trump presidency, and other developments.

During their conversation at a hotel restaurant near the MLA convention, Stavans agrees with Leal about the crucial function of criticism to the health of a democracy. But he goes on to formulate what might be his most explicit credo about the role of the intellectual: "I agree with his [Leal's] propositions," Stavans declares, "but believe the critic also to be a thermometer of cultural heat." He goes on to describe that thermometer at some length:

> His responsibility is to ponder ideas big and small, to speak truth to power, to reach out into different disciplines, to be a fearless generalist, to make his message through various genres (the essay, translation, fiction, poetry, political speeches), to engage in media (television, radio, film, Internet), and to leave a record for future generations of the changes under way in his own time. To me, by definition, the literary critic needs to become a cultural commentator. This is because literature no longer holds a privileged place in society. It has been replaced by more nervous media: television, movies, Internet. The critic's duty is to be always on the move, to be an *arriviste*. And since that approach forces him to constantly reinvent himself, to borrow interpreting tools from others he is also an impostor and an interloper. (*Luis Leal Reader* x)

That "fearless generalist" who engages with various genres and media in order to leave a record of cultural changes in his own time is an idealized portrait of Ilan Stavans himself. Aside from political speeches (unlike Pablo Neruda, a Chilean senator whom he cherishes for having written some poems that "are of such inspired beauty as to justify the very existence of the Spanish language" ["Disturbing Pablo Neruda's Rest"], Stavans has not—yet—run for office), he has expressed himself in every medium he mentions: essay, translation, fiction, television, radio, film, and internet. Despite claiming: "I have never been a serious reader of poetry" (*On Borrowed Words* 228), he has translated Felipe Alfau, Yehuda Amichai, Elizabeth Bishop, Rubén Darío, Emily Dickinson, Yehuda Halevi, Pablo Neruda, and César Vallejo and edited *The FSG Book of 20th-Century Latin American Poetry* (2011), all of which required some serious reading of poetry. He even published a poem he himself wrote, "Our Dreams," in the May 3, 2016, daily blog of *Tikkun* magazine.

Stavans admits that "as I young man, I thoroughly disliked poetry. I didn't see a reason for it" (Dueben). However, by 2018, he was able to describe his evolution as a serious reader—and writer—of poetry as culminating in the fact that "today I can do without the color yellow but not without poetry" (Dueben). Though he has not abjured lemons, bananas, or mustard, he finally, at age fifty-six, did publish an entire volume of poetry, a book-length poem called *The Wall*. Incited by President Trump's grandiose project of constructing an insurmountable barricade stretching from Brownsville to San Diego, it is a Whitmanesque account of an epic journey along the 1,959-mile border between Mexico and the United States. Stavans cites the distance as 1,959 miles, although the International Boundary and Water Commission measures it at 1,954 miles (International Boundary and Water Commission). His encyclopedic ambitions are underlined by code-switching between English and Spanish and, occasionally, Arabic, French, and Hebrew. The poem begins by recalling the partition erected between seven-year-old Ilan and his five-year-old brother to create separate bedrooms for the two boys and expands into a meditation on the inhumanity of barriers built in Beijing, Berlin, Jerusalem, Warsaw, and within the human heart. The 120-page book, published by the University of Pittsburgh Press as part of its prestigious Pitt Poetry Series, strengthens Stavans's credentials as a fearless generalist.

Though his commitment to poetry was somewhat belated, Stavans has never left any doubt about his interest in fiction. However, he has also admitted: "I really don't like reading long novels" (*Quixote* 209). Nevertheless, he apparently likes reading *Don Quixote*, *One Hundred Years of Solitude*, *Madame Bovary*, and *Moby-Dick* enough to wax rhapsodically about those and other long novels. Though itemizing his varied enterprises, even poetry, might make Stavans sound smug and preening, he reiterates his call for restless movement and constant reinvention. He also tries to recuperate as virtues what others charge as faults, that he is an impostor and an interloper.

Ultimately, Stavans's *academic/intellectual* binary is simplistic and self-serving. Given a choice between myopic drudge and universal genius, who would choose the former? But, in a universe of accidents, few are granted that clear a choice. Furthermore, foxes need hedgehogs, as much as hedgehogs need foxes. Those who would serve as bridges require something to connect. The laws of cultural economy permit only a few academics—Stanley Fish, Camille Paglia, Cornel West, Ilan Stavans—to engage much of the general public. But in the heart of every academic beats the soul of a frustrated intellectual—just as every honest intellectual who gazes into the mirror beholds an impostor and an interloper.

8 ILAN STAVANS TONGUE SNATCHER

> the reality beyond language is not completely
> reality, a reality that does not speak or say is not
> reality; and the moment I say that, the moment
> I write, letter by letter, that a reality stripped of
> names is not reality, the names evaporate, they
> are air, they are a sound encased in another
> sound and in another and another, a murmur,
> a faint cascade of meanings that fade away to
> nothingness.
>
> —Octavio Paz (*Monkey Grammarian* 52)

In 1772, Johann Gottfried Herder dubbed our species *Homo loquens*—Talking Man—as if language were the distinguishing feature of what it is to be human (Herder). Some ethologists disagree, insisting that other species also employ sophisticated systems of communication that could qualify as language. Regardless of whether chimpanzees, bonobos, dolphins, birds, bees, and other animals also perform linguistic acts, Stavans insists that language defines his own personal identity. Convinced that "without language I am nobody" (*On Borrowed Words* 250), Stavans is somebody who makes language central to almost everything he writes, especially his autobiography, largely an account of his migration among Yiddish, Spanish, Hebrew, and English and aptly titled *On Borrowed Words*. Language is clearly the hero of his books on dictionaries, Hebrew, and Spanglish, but it is also at issue when he discusses such disparate matters as censorship, the Bible, Jewishness, and love. Faced with a philosophical question, Stavans responds immediately by looking up the meaning of the word in the *Oxford English Dictionary*—"It is a masterpiece of epic proportions, and its views of the universe permeate everything" (*Knowledge and Censorship* 74), he contends. Thus, in *Love & Language* (2007), he begins successive discussions of key concepts, including *melodrama* (8), *love* (13), *desire* (42), *lust* (43), *kiss* (48), *beauty* (120), *taste* (129), *perversion* (151), and *nationalism* (225), by citing the definition and often the etymology supplied by the *OED*.

Behind Stavans's logophilia lies a belief in linguistic determinism, a conviction—known among linguists as the Sapir–Whorf hypothesis—that language constructs weltanschauung and defines identity. Martin Heidegger provided its philosophical formulation: "Language is not a mere tool which man possesses; on the contrary, it is only language that affords the very possibility of standing in the openness of the existent. Only where there is language, is there world, i.e., the perpetually altering circuit of decision and production, of action and responsibility, but also of commotion and arbitrariness, of decay and confusion" (Heidegger, "Hölderlin and the Essence" 276). ("Die Sprache is nicht ein verfügbares Werkzeug, sondern dasjenige Ereignis, das über die höchste Möglichkeit des Menschseins verfügt. Nur wo Sprache, da ist Welt, der stats sich wandelnde Umkreis von Entschediung und Werk, von Tat und Verantwortung, aber auch von Willkür und Lärm, Vergall und Verwirrung" [Heidegger *Erläuterungen* 38]). So if "Nur wo Sprache, da ist Welt" (Only where there is language, is there world), then the most vibrant world is one sustained by the most sophisticated use of language. Fond of quoting Ludwig Wittgenstein's maxims on the sovereignty of language, Stavans states: "I've defined my life in the last few years by his statements that the limit of our language is the limit of our world and that whatever cannot be said doesn't exist" (*Love & Language* 235).

Most linguists conclude that particular languages do not determine particular thoughts but rather incline us toward them. However, Stavans states unequivocally: "I firmly believe that how one perceives the world in any given moment depends on the language in which that moment is experienced" ("On Self-Translation"). Discussing how the Pirahã of the Amazon lack verb forms for future and past tenses, he argues that their language therefore imprisons them in a conceptual present. "History is only possible in a civilization that uses a language capable of tense and aspect," he maintains (*Knowledge and Censorship* 8). Adopting an extreme form of linguistic determinism, Stavans contends that the breadth of our universe is dictated by the scope of our language and that if something cannot be put into words it does not exist: "El tamaño de neustro universe está dictado por el alcance de nuestro lenguaje; solo existe lo que puede ser dicho" (Stavans and Zurita 65).

Wary of limiting his world, Stavans chafes at the limitations of language. If there is no escape from what Frederic Jameson, echoing Friedrich Nietzsche, called "the prison-house of language" (Jameson), we must at least try to make that house as spacious as possible. Because, according to Stavans, "Monolinguals are imprisoned in a single-channeled existence" (*Knowledge and Censorship* 92), he has been an energetic champion and exemplar of multilingualism. For him, as for Johann Wolfgang von Goethe, only the polyglot can truly speak any language; as Goethe put it, "Wer fremde Sprachen nicht kennt weiss nichts von seiner eigenen" (Those ignorant of any foreign language know nothing of their own) (Goethe 508). Stavans repeatedly notes that Jewish culture has long expressed itself through numerous symbiotic languages, and he scolds American Jews for retreating into the insularity of a single tongue, English: "Looking back," he says, "there must not be many powerful, potent Jewish communities in history that have been so frighteningly monolingual as the American Jews are" (*Singer's Typewriter* 291–92). If language inevitably entails both articulation and incarceration, the polyglot at least inhabits a more commodious prison-house.

By choosing their vocation, writers sentence themselves to the pen—writing implement and linguistic penitentiary. "Language is the only—the true—home of the writer" (Wassner 492), Stavans declares. When that home is flimsy, the experience can be unsettling. When Stavans settled in New York, his command of the local language was shaky at best—limited to a lexicon of no more than one hundred words. He recalls that "my English was ridiculous, if it was anything at all. I had the skills of a two-year-old: I could babble, hoping to be understood" (*On Borrowed Words* 10). He had already been writing in Spanish and Yiddish, but, at age twenty-four, if he wanted to pursue his literary ambitions in the United States, he had to improve his command of English beyond the level of a prattler.

An interview with the Peruvian writer Isaac Goldemberg, who "had been living in New York for over two decades without mastering the English language because he did not want his Spanish to suffer and ultimately evaporate" (*Inveterate Dreamer* 261), provided a decisive impetus. Goldemberg's example crystallized Stavans's determination to pursue the opposite course: "I would perfect my English and thus become a New York Jew, an intellectual animal in the proud tradition celebrated by Alfred Kazin" (*Inveterate Dreamer* 261–62). It is a moment similar to the conclusion of Balzac's *Père Goriot*, in which ambitious young Eugène de Rastignac stands on a cemetery hill overlooking the early evening lights of Paris and, determined to conquer the city, vows: "A nous deux, maintenant!" Stavans confronted the translingual challenge, of learning to write in a language other than his primary ones. And he did it within five years. However, a memory of his grandmother adds a cautionary note to the triumphalism of language acquisition. In *On Borrowed Words*, Stavans recalls how Bobbe Bela shared with her grandson the thirty-seven-page memoir she had composed. He notes that it is filled with inaccuracies and distortions, perhaps because she composed it in fractured Spanish rather than Russian, Polish, or Yiddish, languages in which she was more comfortable.

Stavans often refers to himself as quadrilingual, adept, to varying degrees, in Yiddish, Spanish, Hebrew, and English. Raised in Mexico City by a family that spoke Yiddish and Spanish, he explains, "I have two mother tongues—*di mame loshen* and *la lengua materna*" ("On Self-Translation"). He attended a Jewish day school in which Yiddish was the language of instruction and Hebrew was also taught, earned a BA at the Hispanophone Universidad Autónoma Metropolitana, strengthened his command of Hebrew during a year spent in Israel, and became fluent in English after settling in the United States. "For me language is home," he told Carlos Fonseca Suárez, a novelist who, born in Costa Rica, raised in Puerto Rico, and resident in London, shares Stavans's extraterritoriality. "The true home of the writer is language," Stavans insists. "In that sense, I have not one but several homes: Yiddish, Spanish, Hebrew, and English" (Stavans and Fonseca). However, earlier in his career, before becoming a citizen of the United States in 1994, he described his condition as linguistic homelessness, in which "no language—neither Spanish nor English—is truly my own" (*Riddle of Cantinflas* 115). The declaration seems more a matter of pride than despair, a cosmopolitan's assertion of creative estrangement rather than a plaint over deprivation.

Yet, for the most part, Stavans contends that his four languages are as integral as body organs to defining who he is. "Spanish is my right eye," he says (perhaps echoing the admonition in Matthew 5:39 "And if thy right eye offend thee, pluck it out"), "English my left; Yiddish my background and Hebrew my conscience" (*One-Handed Pianist* 182). He repeated the quip—"Spanish is my right eye, English my left; Yiddish my background and Hebrew my conscience (*Inveterate Dreamer* 254)—verbatim in a later book. Elsewhere, he told an interviewer: "By accident, I'm a Spanish speaker. My roots are in Yiddish. Hebrew is my future and English my present" (Wassner 492). Stavans originally planned to compose part of his autobiography, *On Borrowed Words*, in each of his four languages (*Singer's Typewriter* 292–93), but that was as impractical as the strategy William Faulkner's publisher forced him to jettison his ambition to print each chapter of *The Sound and the Fury* in a different color ink. According to the Romantic linguist Wilhelm von Humboldt, each language possesses its own distinctive genius, a unique worldview: "So liegt in jeder Sprache eine eigenthümliche Weltansicht" (Humboldt 224). If so, each of Stavans's four languages—Spanish, English, Yiddish, and Hebrew—would impose a different template on experience, inclining its user to apprehend the world in a unique way. Convinced that speaking Spanish situates the speaker differently in the world than speaking Yiddish, Stavans insists that "eating in Spanish—dreaming, loving, and deriving meaning from life in that language—all these actions differ from their counterparts in Yiddish. The taste of things is determined by the words used to express it" ("On Self-Translation"). If so, then the fact that he made that statement in English shaped it in ways that Spanish and Yiddish would not have.

According to legend, the Holy Roman Emperor Charles V declared: "Je parle espagnol à Dieu, italien aux femmes, français aux hommes, et allemand à mon cheval" (I speak Spanish to God, Italian to women, French to men, and German to my horse). Similarly, Stavans assigns a specific function to each of his languages: "English is best for essays and lectures, Spanish for writing fiction and expressing emotion, Yiddish is unparalleled when it comes to offensive words, and Hebrew is unparalleled for etymological disquisitions" (*Knowledge and Censorship* 65–66). He did indeed write two books of fiction, *La pianista manca* (1992) and *Talia y el cielo* (1989), in Spanish, the tongue he finds "incredibly elastic and suitable to engage in daydreaming" (*Knowledge and Censorship* 66). As a clever schoolboy at the Colegio Israelita de México, he no doubt used Yiddish for offensive words, but early in his career, in 1979, he also used that language to write a musical, *Genesis 2000*, that is derived from Antoine de Saint-Exupéry's *Le Petit Prince* and that he would later dismiss as "a piece of juvenilia" (Sokol 19). Stavans has also employed Spanglish, the demotic hybrid of Spanish and English that he has become a champion of, to translate the first chapter of *Don Quixote* and a scene from *Hamlet*. In 2016, he returned to his childhood favorite to produce *El Little Príncipe*, a versión of Saint-Exupéry's book in Spanglish. Lest the decision to market *Le Petit Prince* in Spanglish seem particularly remarkable, it should be noted that Stavans's publisher, Tintenfass, located in Germany, has also brought out separate editions of the French classic in more than three dozen other unlikely languages, including Hawaiian, Mayan, Old English, Pashto, Provencal, Sanskrit, and Welsh. They have even published versions in Morse code and Egyptian hieroglyphics.

However, Stavans used English to write his book on Hebrew, and English is the language he uses there and elsewhere to examine etymologies. Though he might consider it "my future," Hebrew, in which he has not published any books, is the one of his four languages that in past and present seems least developed. *Resurrecting Hebrew* (2008), which begins with a dream in which an attractive woman speaks in Hebrew to an uncomprehending Stavans, is in fact as much about his own guilt over the fact that he has allowed his command of the language to atrophy as it is about the extraordinary revival of the ancient Jewish language for widespread modern use.

Stavans is a prominent example of a translingual writer, that is, a writer who writes in more than one language or a language other than his or her primary one (Kellman, *Translingual*). Translingual literature has an ancient pedigree, stretching perhaps as far back as the twenty-third century BCE, when the first poet history knows by name, Enheduanna, the only daughter of the powerful Akkadian king Sargon, wrote in Sumerian, though her first language was probably Akkadian. It is quite possible that Anatolians, Carthaginians, Etruscans, and other peoples of the Mediterranean basin and Asia Minor appropriated the newly devised alphabet introduced to them by the seafaring Phoenicians not only by adapting it to their own unlettered tongues but also by writing in Phoenician. Under Roman rule, Apuleius, Ausonius, Lucan, Martial, Quintillian, Seneca, and Terence wrote in Latin, the empire's dominant language, though—like the immigrant Stavans in the New York metropolis—they were outlanders from distant provinces. Medieval and Renaissance writers such as Petrarch, Desiderius Erasmus, and Thomas More also adopted Latin instead of or in addition to their vernaculars. Similarly, Arabic, Chinese, Greek, Persian, and Sanskrit hegemony encouraged translingualism.

Among modern authors, the most celebrated examples of translingualism are Samuel Beckett, Joseph Conrad, and Vladimir Nabokov. Stavans is fascinated by the phenomenon of literary translingualism—what, in an early essay collected in *Art and Anger* (1996), he calls "tongue snatching" ("the art of switching from one language to another" [204])—and is inspired by his own ability as a writer to navigate among Spanish, English, and Spanglish. However, he makes only passing reference to Beckett, Conrad, and Nabokov. Yet, while returning repeatedly to his "idols" Spinoza and Kafka, both of whom wrote in adopted languages, he discusses at length the translingual cases of Julia Alvarez, Hector Biancotti, Joseph Brodsky, Elias Canetti, Judith Ortiz Cofer, Ariel Dorfman, Rosario Ferré, Albert Gerchunoff, Fernando Pessoa, Richard Rodriguez, and George Steiner. Isaiah Berlin switched languages from Russian to English, and Stavans, who named his second child after him and proudly states that he keeps a portrait of him in his office (Sokol 74), insists that few modern thinkers are "as stimulating, coherent, and lucid as Berlin" (*Critic's Journey* 172). Felipe Alfau, a native of Barcelona who moved to the United States at age fourteen, was one of the first Spaniards to write fiction in English, and Stavans was instrumental in reviving interest in the two innovative, neglected novels—*Locos: A Comedy of Gestures* (1936) and *Chromos* (1990)—that Alfau wrote in English. Stavans interviewed the nonagenarian Alfau in his nursing home in Queens, began researching a biography of Alfau that he never completed, and translated into English *La poesía cursi*, a collection of poems that Alfau wrote in Spanish.

Alfau begins *Chromos* with a sentence underlining the challenge of translingualism: "The moment one learns English, complications set in" (7). It is a statement that surely resonates with Stavans, who, after arriving in New York, struggled to master English thoroughly enough to make a career writing in it. His own successful tongue-snatching is as dramatic as the translingual transformations of writers he has studied and admired. While language does not entirely limit thought (it is possible, though more difficult, for an Anglophone Floridian to think as lucidly about snow as the speaker of a Sami language), it does focus attention. The fact that the Pirahã of Brazil speak a language devoid of words for color does not mean that their eyes lack cone cells, only that they are probably less attentive than English speakers to gradations in the spectrum of light. English speakers, however, can usually ignore the geographical coordinates of North, South, East, and West, unlike speakers of the Australian aboriginal Guugu Yimithirr, which requires spatial positioning of every statement. English has more in common linguistically with Spanish than it does with Yiddish or Hebrew, but among the complications that set in for anyone trying to switch from Spanish to English is the wider vocabulary in mongrel English, an alien phonology, and an often bizarre orthography. Whereas Spanish enforces a binary division of the universe into gender categories (*la casa* and *la revista*, but *el jardin* and *el libro*), modern English allows its speakers to ignore whether a friend is male or female, *amigo* or *amiga*. And modern English, which deals straightforwardly with hypotheticals, lacks Spanish's elaborate system of subjunctives; perhaps it was inevitable that *Don Quixote*, the quintessential account of an imagination obsessed with alternative realities, was written in Castilian.

So, to what extent does the language in which Stavans chooses to write determine the kind of writing he does? A fine measure of linguistic determinism in Stavans's oeuvre would have been available if he had written his memoir *On Borrowed Words* in English and then reconceived it in Spanish. In 1998, after completing his memoir *Heading South, Looking North*, Ariel Dorfman, who describes himself as "a bigamist of language," produced a Spanish version, *Rumbo al Sur, deseando el Norte*, that is not exactly a translation (Kellman "Writing South and North"). Beginning with the different titles (*deseando* means "desiring," not "looking"), Dorfman as self-translator takes liberties that he acknowledges the hired translators of his novels and plays into Italian and Korean would not dare. A different Dorfman is constructed by each linguistic rendition of his life. His ambilingual attention to situating himself within two different communities is apparent in the separate ways he handles cultural references. The English edition includes allusions to such figures of North American popular culture as Yogi Berra, Charlie McCarthy, and *Mad* magazine, whereas the Spanish version targets South American readers and shapes a South American self with references to Bernardo O'Higgins, Cantínflas, and *los pacos* (the Chilean police).

However, Stavans, who wrote his doctoral dissertation from Columbia University, "Mexico y su novela policial," in Spanish, farmed out its English translation, *Antiheroes: Mexico and Its Detective Novel*, to others, Jesse H. Lytle and Jennifer A. Matson. Similarly, he consigned to Juan Fernando Merino the task of translating into Spanish *Quixote: The Novel and the World* and *Gabriel García Márquez: The Early Years*, as *Quijote: La novela y el mundo* (2015), and *Gabriel García Márquez: Los años formativos, 1927–1970* (2015), respectively; to Leticia Barrera the Spanish translation of *On Borrowed Words*, as *Palabras prestadas: Autobiografía* (2013); to Verónica Albin the Spanish translation of *Dictionary Days*, as *Días de diccionario* (2006); and to Sergio M. Sarmiento the Spanish translation of *The Hispanic Condition*, as *La condición hispánica* (2001). Nor did Stavans have a hand in the translations of his works into Chinese, Dutch, French, German, Hebrew, Italian, Japanese, Polish, and Portuguese.

He has written most of his fiction in Spanish, and, except for two slight efforts by the author himself, "The Death of Yankos" and "House Repossessed," all the translations collected in *The One-Handed Pianist and Other Stories*—an English rendition of stories Stavans published in Spanish in *Talia y el cielo* and *La pianista manca*—are credited to others: Dick Gerdes, Harry Morales, Amy Prince, David Unger, and

Stavans's wife, Alison Stavchansky. Stavans explains why he declined the request by his publisher, Viking, to translate *On Borrowed Words* into Spanish himself, instead delegating the task to Leticia Barrera, the wife of a friend: "It would have taken enormous psychological effort to redress the narrative, which I had fashioned with such care, in another language. It would have essentially meant rewriting the book, and repetition is one of my lifelong phobias. Besides, why redo the autobiography when I could employ my energy in other ventures?" ("On Self-Translation"). Among Stavans's other ventures is an entire book, *On Self-Translation: Meditations on Language* (2018), in which he expands on his resistance to reworking his own texts in another language, in addition to expatiating on familiar themes such as dictionaries, language academies, and Spanglish.

Without two versions of the autobiography, it is possible only to speculate about how the fact that Stavans presents his life in English rather than Spanish shapes that life. However, Stavans did note that, though he chose to write his autobiography in English, he adopted the strategy employed by Henry Roth, who fashioned a distinctive English prose to represent the Yiddish that his immigrant characters speak in *Call It Sleep*. Stavans explained:

> In the end, I decided to write the entire autobiography *in translation without an original*, that is, to give my English a variety of accents. And so, for example, I wrote about the Yidishe Schule in Mexike where I studied as a child in English, but used a Yiddish cadence, a rhythm that makes it appear, to invoke Bialik's metaphor, as if one is accessing that period "through a veil." The same goes for my experiences in Israel, where I worked at a kibbutz. I wanted the reader to get the impression that something was awkward, slightly amiss—that the lens through which my odyssey was seen was somewhat warped. ("On Self-Translation")

To emphasize the notion that experience is refracted, if not distorted, in translation, Stavans makes reference to the Hebrew poet Haim Nachman Bialik's often-(mis)quoted adage about the frustrations of translation, that "מי שמכ'ר את ה'הדות בת'רגומה הר' הוא כא'לו מנשק את אמו דרך המטפחת" (He who knows Judaism through translation is like one who kisses his mother through a veil) (Bialik 16). Written in English, *On Borrowed Words* is, according to its author, filtering through a veil episodes of a life lived in other languages.

The content of the account of his schoolboy days is certainly Yiddishe, but the style of the prose, is it *azoy* Yiddish? "The Colegio Israelita de México (aka Der Yiddisher Shule in Mexique), in colonia del Valle, which I attended from kindergarten to high school—a total of fifteen years—embodied the views on history, education, and culture sustained by Bela's immigrant generation. From outside, nothing about the building signaled its Jewishness: it had no lettered signs, no insignias. It must have had more than a thousand children enrolled. Its ideology was decidedly

Bundist: secular in vision, embracing culture as the true religion" (*On Borrowed Words* 81).

Mame loshen that isn't. In terms of syntax, turns of phrase, and word order, there is nothing particularly Yiddish in that passage. Word order it does not invert. It does not resort to Yinglish to recount the boychik's experiences. And why doesn't it substitute questions for statements? The passage was written in English and, though describing a Yiddish-speaking school, it embodies the weltanschauung conveyed by the English language.

Stavans's tongue-snatching has obviously had a profound effect on his career and his life in general. But, while it is hard to gauge precisely what difference it makes that most of his texts are written in English rather than Spanish, it is possible on occasion to sense another language lurking beneath the surface of his English prose. Joseph Conrad (né Teodor Jozef Konrad Nalecz Korzeniowski) wrote all his fiction in English, but there are passages in his novels and stories in which he was probably thinking in either Polish or French and simply transliterating words and expressions into English. Studying the Gallicisms in Conrad's prose, instances in which distinctively French turns of phrase infiltrate the English text, Claude Maisonnat cites, for example, instances in which the word order is more French than English, as in *Suspense*, when Conrad writes "Cosmo saw enter a man," as well as calques, as in *Nostromo*, when instead of using the English idiom "without fanfare," Conrad literally transposes the French "sans tambour ni trompette" into "without drum or trumpet" (Maisonnat).

Stavans admits: "I have a foreign accent in the written page as well" (Sokol 18), and the accent betrays itself in that very sentence with a foreigner's mishandling of English prepositions—a native speaker would be more likely to refer to something *on* the written page. Stavans's prose is spotted with occasional calques that are an obvious—and awkward—transposition from Spanish. Discussing the experience of bright Latino students who are accepted into selective colleges, he writes: "And yet, for that privileged few, excitement soon turns into deception" (*Hispanic Condition* 182). Though he must have been thinking of the Spanish word *decepción*, it is a false cognate of the English word *deception*. What he really means to say is that excitement turns into *disappointment*. Similarly, the Spanish word *desinteresado* could mean either *disinterested* or *uninterested*, but Stavans apparently chose the wrong English equivalent when he wrote about Borges's Middle East poems: "Whoever is interested in the Arab-Israeli conflict won't get an uninterested picture through them" (*Borges* 74). As late as 2018, while trying to describe Latino assimilation, Stavans was still stumbling: "Their entrance to the middle class is steady, though it hasn't occurred at the same speed than it has for other immigrant groups" (*Latinos in the United States* xxv).

Further evidence of linguistic interference in Stavans's prose comes from the

Spanish *escatología*, which could mean either *eschatology* or *scatology*. Since *Don Quixote* is more philosophical than salacious, Stavans clearly should have chosen the latter when, observing that Cervantes's book "surely isn't a dirty novel," he explains, "Eschatology is kept in check" (*Quixote* 52). He was also probably thinking of *escenario*—Spanish for scene or setting—when, writing about Octavio Paz, he states that "the metropolis is the scenario of his best poetry" (*Octavio Paz* 81). He contends that the seventeenth-century lexicographer Sebastián de Covarrubias Orozco was "also a cryptographer, a mortalist, and a translator of Horace into Spanish" (*Quixote* 79), but, since everyone alive is a *mortalist*, he probably means that the author was a *moralist*.

There are also occasional misspellings that testify at least to insufficient vigilance by copyeditors—the French novelist Michel Butor is rendered as "Buttor" (*Inveterate Dreamer* 186), and the American biographer Arnold Rampersad becomes "Rampersand" (*Hispanic Condition* 190). In a poem, Stavans writes, leadenly, that:

Every night, as we close our eyes,

we are out of Egypt,

lead by Moses

onto the Promised Land ("Our Dreams").

His texts also contain solecisms not uncommon to native speakers of English but to which newcomers to the language are more susceptible. For example, he spells Harold Bloom's book *The Western Canon* as if it were a study of weapons (i.e., *Cannon*), rather than masterpieces (Sokol 75), and he discusses an attempt to adapt *Don Quixote* into film as "a multi-nation project lead [*sic*] by Orson Welles" (*Quixote* 161). Tongue snatchers challenge the vigilance of copyeditors.

They can also try the patience of readers averse to coy euphemisms. Apparently allergic to the English word *English*, Stavans much prefers the gassy periphrase *Shakespeare's tongue*. He uses the term dozens of times throughout his writings and at least six times within the covers of a single book, *The Hispanic Condition*. In most cases, *Shakespeare's tongue* is not really what he means, but rather the dominant language of contemporary Americans. For the millions of contemporary Anglophones who lack close acquaintance with the sonnets and plays, their tongue is no longer Shakespeare's, however strong his influence on both literature and language. As a lexicographer and defender of Spanglish, Stavans is certainly aware that living languages are not static, that they change over space and time, so that when he describes how, a newcomer to New York, he vows to "vastly improve my skills in the tongue of Shakespeare" (*On Borrowed Words* 222), he does not really want to sound like Marc Antony, Malvolio, or Macbeth, but rather like his neighbors in late twentieth-century Manhattan. By the time Stavans asserts that Joseph Conrad "became one of the most revered masters of Shakespeare's language" (*Art and An-*

ger 204), the turn of phrase has become an irritating Ilanism. The same is true of his repeated and annoying use of *Cervantes's tongue* in place of *Spanish*. Though he writes about "the varieties of Cervantes's tongue on this side of el Océano Atlántico" (*Spanglish* 38), he surely knows that Cervantes never crossed the Atlantic, and that the language he spoke is almost unrecognizable to millions of Hispanophones four and a half centuries later. It is certainly ludicrous for Stavans to discuss the command that Cesar Chavez, the farm labor organizer who had a spotty education, none in Golden Age Castilian, had of "Cervantes's tongue" (Chavez Introduction ix).

For some translinguals, each language, reserved for its own genre, elicits a distinct personality. The south Indian author Kamala Das wrote her poetry in English and her fiction—under the pen name Madhavikutty—in Malayalam. Stavans writes most of his fiction in Spanish and his nonfiction in English. "I find it strange to write nonfiction in Spanish," he acknowledges. "The precise, concrete, almost mathematical quality of the English language is more inviting to me than Spanish for that type of writing" (Stavans and Gautier 144). The nonfiction that has stirred the most controversy is his book on Spanglish, a hybrid tongue he champions against the sclerotic Castilian enforced by the Real Academia Española de la Lengua. Like the government of Singapore, which has been trying to discourage the use of Singlish, a compound of English, Mandarin, Malay, and Tamil, through its official Speak Good English Movement, the academy in Madrid has attacked Spanglish as a bastard phenomenon that is neither Spanish nor English. It has even launched an advertising campaign to mock Spanglish and suppress its use.

Stavans's nemesis, Cuban-born Roberto González-Echevarría, is no fan of Spanglish. He argues that adoption of the hybrid tongue that is an Anglicization of Spanish "would constitute the ultimate imperialistic takeover, the final imposition of a way of life that is economically dominant but not culturally superior in any sense." Spanglish, "the language of poor Latinos, many of whom are illiterate in both languages," he contends, "stands for marginalization, not liberation" (González Echevarría, "Is 'Spanglish' a Language?"). The eminent Colombian author Alvaro Mutis dismissed Stavans's translation of the first chapter of *Don Quixote* into Spanglish as useless, a peculiar stunt that adds nothing to the original—"una cosa chistosa que no agrega nada al texto" (Hernández).

Stavans begins *Spanglish: The Making of a New American Language* (2003), which he wrote in English, with an erudite survey and defense of the mongrel tongue, but most of the volume consists of an alphabetized lexicon, from "@" to "zumear," of Spanglish words with their English definitions. The book concludes with Stavans's translation of the first chapter of *Don Quixote* into Spanglish. He recognizes an "affinity between Spanglish and Yiddish" (*Spanglish* 44) and that his affection for the former derives from his background in the latter, a similar mishmash of more respectable languages that is favored by hoi polloi but mistrusted and even despised by the guardians of linguistic purity. Compounded of Hebrew, German, Russian, Polish, and other European tongues that wandering Jews came into contact with, Yiddish began, in patriarchal Eastern Europe—what Irving Howe, who titled his 1976 study of first-generation of immigrant American Jews *World of Our Fathers*, might call "the world of our forefathers"—as the jargon of the poor, the uneducated, and women. Its flowering as the medium of remarkable and respectable literary art—in the works of Mendele Moykher Sforim, Sholem Aleichem, and I. L. Peretz— came a few decades before the extinction of most of its speakers. Rich in words connoting both endearment and mockery, the Yiddish lexicon, devoid of terms for tanks, bombs, and torpedoes, is a poor tool for devising military tactics. As with Spanglish, it conveys an outsider's weltanschauung, though if the *pícaro* employs tricks to cope with marginality, the *schlimazel* merely muddles through. Isaac Bashevis Singer's description of Yiddish, the creole that earned him a Nobel Prize, applies as well to Spanglish: "a language of exile, without a land, without frontiers, not supported by any government" (Singer, "Nobel Lecture" 164). According to Yiddish linguist Max Weinreich's familiar quip, a language is a dialect "that possesses an army and a navy" (Weinreich A-362). Lacking even a constabulary, both Yiddish and Spanglish have nothing to defend them but Stavans and other loyal speakers.

There is a fine symmetry to Stavans's multilingualism:

Yiddish • Spanish • English • Spanglish

Two normative, imperial languages sandwiched between a couple of raffish, demotic jargons. (Despite his book on Hebrew, Stavans has not employed that language actively.) Stavans attained renown—and notoriety—by writing in "legitimate" Spanish and English, but he taught what is probably the first formal course devoted entirely to Spanglish at an American institution of higher education—at Amherst in 2000. His emergence in his forties as the leading champion of Spanglish can be seen as a reversion of sorts to his Yiddish childhood, to the embrace of a frowzy *mame loshen*. What links Yiddish and Spanglish is Stavans's enthusiasm for *rascuachismo*, a Chicano colloquialism that, he notes with some disdain, is "ignored by the standard *Diccionario de la Real Academia Española*" (*Bandido* 5). He calls the popular Mexican comedian known as Cantínflas (né Fortino Mario Alonso Moreno Reyes) "the ultimate master of *rascuachismo*" (*Riddle of Cantínflas* 35), and he dubs Oscar "Zeta" Acosta "the king of *rascuachismo, el rey* of bad taste" (*Bandido* 5). Both the actor and the activist share marginal origins, an underdog sensibility, and a talent and propensity for exploding conventions and protocols. To define the vulgar qualities that attract him to both, Stavans quotes Tomás Ybarra-Frausto's seminal 1991 essay "Rasquachismo, a Chicano Sensibility": "To be *rascuache* is to posit a bawdy, spunky consciousness, to seek to subvert and turn ruling paradigms upside down. It is a witty, irreverent, and impertinent posture that recodes and moves outside established boundaries" (*Bandido* 6). Nevertheless, Stavans is repulsed by the boorish, blustering womanizer Donald Trump. His fondness for flamboyant figures who violate the canons of good taste is overcome by echoes of racial purity in Trump's immigration policies and his flirtation with white supremacists.

As examples of the *rascuache*, Ybarra-Frausto cites microwave tamales, velvet portraits of Emiliano Zapata, and the defiantly tacky movie *Born in East L.A.*, but he might also have included Spanglish and Yiddish, languages of the barrio and the shtetl, respectively. Both languages challenge propriety and hierarchy. To speak Spanglish is to thumb one's nose at the Real Academia Española and its presumptuous motto "Limpia, fija y da esplendor" (cleans, fixes, and gives splendor)—just as what impresses critic Neal Gabler about Yiddish is "the way it seemed to bulldoze over politesse" (10). Both Spanglish and Yiddish are anti-elitist languages that embody a working-class cheekiness—indeed chutzpah—toward decorum.

Though Stavans wants to extend the phenomenon to Mexican popular culture, Ybarra-Frausto centers *rasquachismo* (*rascuachismo*) in Chicano life. It is a matter of class—working—and attitude—cheeky. However, as a Chilango immigrant from a middle-class Jewish family, Stavans comes, again and again, to Chicano subjects—Cesar Chavez, Oscar "Zeta" Acosta, Selena Quintanilla, Floyd Salas—as an outsider. Yet, ultimately, in his refusal to accept distinctions between insider and outsider, top dog and underdog, proper and uncouth, his entire career has been a performance of *rascuachismo*. Throughout his oeuvre, Stavans is a pluralist mistrustful of cultural and racial purity and drawn to visions and versions of hybridity. When he writes of *la pureza de sangre*, a relic of Spanish colonialism, it is with repugnance. He rejects purity—in bloodlines as much as language. And he revels in the untidiness of North American society. "Democracy is rowdy and boisterous and insatiable" (Foreword to *Chicano Movement* ix), he notes with approval. In *José Vasconcelos: The Prophet of Race* (2011), Stavans spurns the racial eugenics implicit in Vasconcelos's promotion of *la raza cósmica* (the cosmic race, Mexican identity as an amalgam of all peoples). However, there and elsewhere he is drawn repeatedly to the Mexican philosopher's classic 1925 essay "Mestizaje." In his short book *The United States of Mestizo* (2013), a kind of declaration of interdependence, Stavans proclaims: "By virtue of the cross-fertilization defining the world in its entirety, we're all *mestizos* now, no matter if one comes from Managua, Cairo, or Seoul." He adds that it is not merely a matter of ethnic identity, "it is something far bigger yet less tangible: a state of mind" (36–37).

Moreover, Stavans's attraction toward graphic novels, memoirs, and histories—books that mix words with images—is an extension of his advocacy for *mestizaje*. In their own mingling of the verbal and the visual, *United States of Mestizo, Mr. Spic Goes to Washington, El Iluminado, Angelitos, Latino USA*, and *I Love My Selfie* each embody the hybridization that their author celebrates. They are acts of *métissage* that reject the constraints of literary purity that inspired much of modernism—the "pure music" that eschewed a narrative program and the "pure painting" that rebelled against representation. "La poesía desnuda" of Juan Ramón Jimenez attempts to purge the text of anything not unique to poetry. A belief that poetry should do only that which only poetry can do explains why, according to André Breton in the *Premier Manifeste du Surréalisme*, Paul Valéry declared that he would never write a novel. It would require him to create banal and "unpoetic" fillers such as "La marquise sortit à cinq heures" (The Marquise went out at five o'clock). Stavans is postmodern in his urge to mingle genres and media. And he tosses a raspberry at respectability by mixing high and low in combinations that are proudly *rascuache*. Like his fondness for linguistic creoles, Stavans's mingling of words and images derives from his distaste for boundaries.

If mind is embodied in language, Stavans's mind strains against the constrictions of any single language. The ultimate, ideal extrapolation of the translingual project, the switching from one language to another to another, is panlingualism, the embrace of all languages in one cosmic collective utterance. It is the white noise that is tantamount to silence. Stavans, a utopian who dreams of the no place just at the tip of all our tongues, in fact defines Paradise as "the place where language is no longer needed" (*Dictionary Days* 219).

Meanwhile, afflicted with lexicomania, he surrounds himself with "a sea of dictionaries" (*Dictionary Days* 21) from a wide variety of languages and periods. "I'm in the habit of collecting them the way other people collect stamps, painting, and comic books" (21), he reports, in a dictionary daze. He is a collector and connoisseur of dictionaries who refuses to accept any lexicon as prescriptive or definitive, an aficionado of linguistic miscegenation in Yiddish and Spanglish, and a professor who scorns academicism. A translingual who positions himself within and outside the language of his self-conscious prose, Stavans wages his quixotic battles against demarcations, from both outside and inside cultural and linguistic lines. The founder of a company he calls Restless Books, Ilan Stavans keeps on writing in his restless tongues.

9 CHAMELEON MAN

> The chameleon, who is said to feed upon nothing
> but air, has of all animals the nimblest tongue.
>
> —Jonathan Swift (275)

During one of his conversations with Neal Sokol, Stavans offers the chameleon as an emblem of the Jewish people—because of "its talent to meld into the environment, to disguise itself so as to remain alive" (Sokol 69). He points out that Woody Allen's mock documentary *Zelig* (1983), about an American Jew named Leonard Zelig who blends into his shifting surroundings so thoroughly that he seems to lack a consistent, independent existence, suggests the same equation. However, a similar saurian icon is often applied to another of Stavans's identities: the Latino. The title that Delia Poey and Virgil Suarez chose to give the anthology of recent Latino short stories that they edited is, appropriately, *Iguana Dreams: New Latino Fiction* (1992). Following Octavio Paz and Julio Cortázar, Stavans himself seizes on the axolotl, also known as the Mexican salamander, as "the ad hoc symbol of the Hispanic psyche, always in profound mutation, not the mythical creature capable of withstanding fire, but an eternal mutant" (*Hispanic Condition* 13). When he calls Domingo F. Sarmiento, the wily author of *Facundo* who survived political exile to serve as president of Argentina from 1868 to 1874, "the ultimate chameleon" (Introduction to *Facundo* xxxii), he does not mean that Sarmiento was the last one. Or that Stavans disapproves.

Stavans in fact attributes the qualities of a chameleon to both Jews and Latinos and to the Jews of Latin America. He concludes his Introduction to his anthology *The Scroll and the Cross: 1,000 Years of Jewish-Hispanic Literature* by emphasizing the resiliency of Jewish writers in Latin America: "They are Jews in their tradition, in their culture, in their religion; but they struggle to fit into the environment, and in so doing, they incorporate elements of it into their identity. Their prose and poetry is an invaluable testimony of their chameleon-like qualities" (28). For Stavans, both Jew and Latino are unstable categories because each survives and thrives by adapting.

Mexican poet José Emilio Pacheco's first novel, *Morirás lejos* (1967) (*You Will Die Far Away*), ponders the persecution of Jews throughout the centuries. But when one of his poems declares: "El axolotl es nuestro emblema" (Pacheco 32)—"Our emblem is the axolotl" (33)—Pacheco is not evoking the fluctuations of Diasporic history that have required Jews to adjust to hostile and radically changing circumstances. Instead, he finds in the indigenous creature the fitting embodiment of a tenacious indigenous people who have survived the Spanish conquest and much else by accommodating. The axolotl, according to Pacheco,

> ... encarna
> el temor de ser nadie y replegarse
> a la noche perpetua en que los dioses
> se pudren bajo el lago y su silencio
> es oro (Pacheco 32).

> ... embodies
> the dread of being nobody at all, lapped
> back into the perpetual night, where the gods
> rot under the lake, and their silence
> is golden" (Pachecho 33).

Paz's gloss on that would be to note, as he does in *El laberinto de la soledad* (1950) (*The Labyrinth of Solitude*), that *el disimulo*, dissimulation, is the Mexican's survival strategy, that as a result: "We change from somebody into nobody, into nothingness. And this nothingness takes on its own individuality, with a recognizable face and figure, and suddenly becomes Nobody" (Paz 45). Paz might also be describing Leonard Zelig.

Paz himself wrote a twenty-stanza poem, "Salamandra," that is a direct address to the axolotl, invoking fiery imagery to confound the reptile with Xolotl, the Aztec god of fire. And in Cortázar's most famous short story, "Axolotl," a man recounts his obsession with the Mexican salamanders in the aquarium of the Jardin des Plantes in Paris. He returns day after day to gaze at a particular axolotl, until he trades places with the amphibian. He is transformed into the axolotl, the axolotl into him. In his Introduction to a collection of Cortázar's short fiction, Stavans calls "Axolotl" one of his favorite stories. He explains its appeal by stating: "Look carefully and you'll realize that the self is less stable in its presentation than we tend to think; in fact it is in constant mutation, never static, always in the act (and art) of becoming" (Introduction to *Hopscotch* vii). If so, *The Essential Ilan Stavans* can exist only in a state of perpetual revision.

The metamorphosis of the axolotl is something that speaks to Stavans. Discussing "the never-ending mutability of the human self," he reveals: "Not surprisingly, my favorite animals since childhood have been amphibians, creatures of two habitats" (Sokol 68). William Butler Yeats, who adopted occult practices, cautioned himself against splintered identity, lest he find himself "astray upon the Path of the

Chameleon, upon *Hodos Chamelonis*" (Yeats 215). However, Stavans gladly chooses the Path of the Chameleon over the stasis of the sloth. His praise for Neruda's poetry as "fluid, rambunctious, centrifugal" (Preface to *I Explain* xvi) reveals his own propensities. When he wants to praise Roberto Bolaño, who, like Stavans himself, "didn't hold academic life in any esteem" (*Critic's Journey* 143), he declares: "I've never come across a chameleon talent like Bolaño's" (*Critic's Journey* 139). A fox and not a hedgehog, he honors Heraclitus rather than Parmenides, Dionysus rather than Apollo. Though there is a continuity in the Jewish and Latino themes that shape his oeuvre, he is an elusive *pícaro* who exasperates his adversaries because he is as difficult to pin down as the shape-shifter Proteus.

For page after page, Stavans's work can sometimes seem like an information drop, substituting a parade of erudition for genuine elucidation. However, because much of what he has to say is delivered in conversations and interviews, his thoughts are dialectical, not definitive. Those eager to argue with his conclusions are exasperated by their absence. His texts are defined more by the journey than any destination. Refusing to play by the rules of academic discourse, he is a trickster, an outsider who has mastered the language of the insiders.

Stavans has attracted many admirers—and detractors—but no disciples. There is no School of Stavans. Because Amherst College has no doctoral program, he lacks a pipeline of protégés. And, because he eschews intellectual systems, his books are rarely systematic. Because his writing is often ad hoc, occasioned by commissions and events, it would be foolhardy to predict the directions he will take.

Letters are a passion for the *hombre de letras*. However, despite Stavans's obsession with dictionaries and his preoccupation with his own translingualism, there are limits to his verbolatry. Lurking beneath his zest for expressing himself in the right words is a profound pessimism, even nihilism, about the enduring power of literature, since, as he puts it, "words are transient, inaccurate . . . light as smoke" (*¡Muy Pop!* 1). In his graphic books, he moves beyond words. More fundamentally, in his darker moments, he confronts in words what he calls "the abyss that is life" (Stavans and Gracia 14). Stavans's strategy for staving off despair is to keep hurling books into that abyss. Analyzing the design of Ernesto Galarza's memoir *Barrio Boy*, he notes: "The narrative is packaged as a series of connected facts organized to persuade the reader that life is coherent, sequential, and meaningful." It is nothing of the sort, he contends. "It is messy, hectic, empty of any rationale." But, like an earnest Existentialist, he hastens to add: "We, who live it, inject it with a purpose" (Introduction to *Barrio Boy* xv). The serum that Stavans—insider/outsider—injects is words, words, words. Nevertheless, by the time he came to write an essay about his father's dementia, in 2018, he was conceding that even words fail him: "Because no matter how strenuously we battle against it, oblivion always prevails" ("Friday Takeaway: Forgetting").

WORKS CITED

Abdel-Maggid, Yassmin. "As Lionel Shriver Made Light of Identity, I Had No Choice but to Walk Out on Her." *Guardian*, September 20, 2016. https://www.theguardian.com /commentisfree/2016/sep/10/as-lionel-shriver-made-light-of-identity-i-had-no-choice -but-to-walk-out-on-her.

Alfau, Felipe. *Chromos.* Normal, IL: Dalkey Archive Press, 1990.

Alfau, Felipe. *Locos: A Comedy of Gestures.* New York: Farrar and Rinehart, 1936.

Alfau, Felipe. *Sentimental Songs: La poesía cursi.* Bilingual edition. Translated with an introduction by Ilan Stavans. Normal, IL: Dalkey Archive Press, 1992.

Allatson, Paul. "Ilan Stavans's *Latino USA: A Cartoon History* (Of a Cosmopolitan Intellectual)." *Chasqui* 35, no. 2 (2006): 21–41.

Baal-Makhshoves. "One Literature in Two Languages." Translated by Hana Wirth-Nesher. In *Switching Languages: Translingual Writers Reflect on Their Craft*, edited by Steven G. Kellman, 97–109. Lincoln: University of Nebraska Press, 2003.

Barra, Allen. *Yogi Berra: Eternal Yankee.* New York: Norton, 2010.

Barthes, Roland. *Le Degré zéro de l'écriture: suivi de Éléments de sémiologie.* Paris: Gonthier, 1953.

Bialik, H. N. "Al Umah ve-Lashon." *Devarim she-be-al Peh*, vol. 1, 15–20. Tel Aviv: Dvir, 1935.

Boswell, James. *Life of Samuel Johnson, L.L.D. and Journal of His Tour to the Hebrides.* Edited by Henry Morley. New York: George Routledge and Sons, 1885.

Boyd, Brian. *Vladimir Nabokov: The American Years.* Princeton, NJ: Princeton University Press, 1991.

Breton, André. *Manifestes du Surréalisme.* Paris: J. J. Pauvert, 1962.

Browne, Ray B. *Against Academia: The History of the Popular Culture Association / American Culture Association and The Popular Culture Movement 1967–1988.* Bowling Green, OH: Bowling Green State University Popular Press, 1989.

Carbajo, Juan A. "El Mundo hispánico hablará spanglish." *El País*, January 2, 2000. http:// elpais.com/diario/2000/01/02/cultura/946767601850215.html.

Carroll, Lewis. *Alice's Adventures in Wonderland and Through the Looking Glass.* New York: Penguin, 1998.

Cashman, Holly R. "Stavans, Ilan. *Spanglish: The Making of a New American Language.*" *Chasqui* 34, no. 1 (2005): 216–19.

Chavez, Cesar. *An Organizer's Tale: Speeches.* Edited with an introduction by Ilan Stavans. New York: Penguin, 2008.

Cheyette, Bryan. "To Be Discontinued." *TLS*, April 30, 1999, 25.

Christophersen, Bill. "Review of *The One-Handed Pianist and Other Stories*." *New York Times Book Review*, May 5, 1996, 22.

Darío, Rubén. *Rubén Darío: Selected Writings*. Edited by Ilan Stavans. New York: Penguin, 2005.

Dueben, Alex. "Smash Pages Q&A: Ilan Stavans." *Smash Pages: The Comics Super Blog*, February 27, 2018. http://smashpages.net/2018/02/27/smash-pages-qa-ilan-stavans/.

Dundas, Deborah. "Editor Quits amid Outrage after Call for 'Appropriation Prize' in Writers' Magazine." *Toronto Star*, May 10 2017. https://www.thestar.com/entertainment/books/2017/05/10/editor-quits-amid-outrage-after-call-for-appropriation-prize-in-writers-magazine.htm.

Durán, Isabel. "Ethics and Aesthetics: A Conversation with Ilan Stavans." *Camino Real* 6, no. 9 (2014): 145–61.

Einstein, Albert. "'Primitiver Aberglaube': Einstein über Religion." *Humanistischer Pressdienst*, May 16, 2008. https://hpd.de/node/4584.

Erasmus, Desiderius. *Praise of Folly*. Translated by Betty Radice. New York: Penguin, 1993.

Feinberg, Richard. "Stranger: The Challenge of a Latino Immigrant in the Trump Era." *Foreign Affairs* 97, no. 3 (2018): 199–200.

Folsom, Raphael. "Review *of Art and Anger* and *Imagining Columbus*." *Hispanic American Historical Review* 83, no. 2 (2003): 361–63.

Foster, David William. "Review of *Ilan Stavans: Eight Conversations*." *Hispania* 89, no. 1 (2006): 73–74.

Fowler, H.W., and F. G. Fowler. *The King's English*. Oxford: Clarendon Press, 1922.

Gabler, Neal. Introduction to *Yiddishkeit*, edited by Harvey Pekar and Paul Buhle, 9–10. New York: Abrams Comicarts, 2011.

Galarza, Ernesto. *Barrio Boy: 40th Anniversary Edition*. Introduction by Ilan Stavans. Notre Dame, IN: University of Notre Dame Press, 2011.

Gallo, Rubén. "Octavio Paz, A Meditation de Ilán Stavans." *Revista Iberoamericana* 69, no. 205 (2003): 1037–40.

Gessner, Niklaus. *Die Unzulänglichkeit der Sprache: Eine Untersuchung* über *Formzerfall und Beziehungslosigkeit bei Samuel Beckett*. Zurich: Juris, 1957.

Goethe, Johann Wolfgang von. *Goethes Werk: Schriften zur Kunst, Schriften zur Literatur, Maximen und Reflexionen*. Vol. 12, edited by Erich Truns and Hans Joachim Schrimpf. Munich: C. H. Beck, 1981.

González, Juan. *Harvest of Empire: A History of Latinos in America*. New York: Penguin, 2000.

González Echevarría, Roberto. "Is 'Spanglish' a Language? Hispanics Should Learn English and Proper Spanish. *New York Times*, March 28, 1997.

González Echevarría, Roberto. "The Master of Modernismo." *The Nation*, January 25, 2006. https://www.thenation.com/article/master-modernismo/.

Gracia, Jorge J. E. *Latinos in America: Philosophy and Social Identity.* Malden, MA: Blackwell, 2008.

Grenier, Yvon. "Octavio Paz: An Intellectual and His Critics." *Mexican Studies* 21, no. 1 (2005): 251–67.

Gruesz, Kirsten Silva. "What Was Latino Literature?" *PMLA* 127, no. 2 (2012): 335–41.

Gutierrez, David G. "Ethnic Labels, Latino Lives: Identity and the Politics of (Re)Presentation in the United States / The Hispanic Condition: Reflections on Culture and Identity in America." *Journal of American Ethnic History* 17, no. 1 (1997): 99–101.

Heidegger, Martin. *Erläuterungen zu Hölderlins Dichtung.* Frankfurt am Main: Vittorio Klostermann, 1981.

Heidegger, Martin. "Hölderlin and the Essence of Poetry." Translated by D. Scott, in Heidegger, *Existence and Being.* Chicago: H. Regnery, 1949.

Heller, Scott. "'Living in the Hyphen' Between Latin and American." *Chronicle of Higher Education* 44, no. 18 (January 9, 1998): A17–A18.

Herder, Johann Gottfried. "On the Origin of Language." In Jean-Jacques Rousseau and Johann Gottfried Herder, *On the Origin of Language.* Translated by John H. Moran and Alexander Gode. Chicago: University of Chicago Press, 1966.

Hernández, Edgar Alejandro. "'Buena idea,' pero . . . ¿quién va a leer?" *Mural* (Guadalajara), July 1, 2002, p. 9.

Hirsch, Edward. "James Salter, The Art of Fiction No. 133." *Conversations with James Salter,* edited by Jennifer Levasseur and Kevin Rabalais, 35–64. Jackson: University Press of Mississippi, 2015.*Hopscotch: A Cultural Review.* https://muse.jhu.edu/journal/73.

Howe, Irving. *World of Our Fathers; The Journey of the East European Jews to America and the Life They Found and Made.* New York: Harcourt Brace Jovanovich, 1976.

Humboldt, Wilhelm von. "Über die Versciedenheit des menschlichen Sprachhaus." *Schriften zur Sprachphilosophie,* vol. 3. Darmstadt: Wissenschafliche Buchgesellschaft, 1963.

International Boundary and Water Commission. United States and Mexico. United States Section. https://www.ibwc.gov/AboutUs/AboutUs.html.

Italie, Hillel. "Disputed Book Pulled from Oprah Web Site." Associated Press, November 6, 2007. http://www.washingtonpost.com/wp-dyn/content/article/2007/11/06/AR2007110601431.html.

Jacoby, Russell. *The Last Intellectuals: American Culture in the Age of Academe.* New York: Basic Books, 1987.

Jameson, Frederic. *The Prison-house of Language: A Critical Account of Structuralism and Russian Formalism.* Princeton, NJ: Princeton University Press, 1972.

Jason, Philip K. "Fate Knocking at the Door: An Interview with Ilan Stavans." Jewish Book Council, December 19, 2012. http://www.jewishbookcouncil.org/book/singers-type writer-and-mine#Interview.

Johnson, Greg, ed. *Joyce Carol Oates: Conversations, 1970–2006.* Princeton, NJ: Ontario Review Press, 2006.

Jonson, Ben. *Timber: or, Discoveries.* Vol. 8, *Ben Jonson.* Edited by C. H. Herford and Percy and Evelyn Simpson. Oxford: Oxford University Press, 1925–1952.

Joyce, James. *A Portrait of the Artist as a Young Man.* New York: Bantam Dell, 2005.

Juvenal. Satire VII. *Juvenal and Persius.* Translated by G. G. Ramsay, 136–57. New York: G. P. Putnam's Sons, 1918.

Kafka, Franz. *The Diaries: 1910–1923.* Edited by Max Brod, translated by Joseph Kresh and Martin Greenberg, with the cooperation of Hannah Arendt. New York: Schocken, 2000.

Kameli, Marziyeh. "An Interview with Ilan Stavans." *Los Angeles Review of Books,* January 10, 2017. https://lareviewofbooks.org/article/interview-ilan-stavans/.

Kelley, Rich. "The Library of America Interviews Ilan Stavans about *Becoming Americans.*" *Library of America e-Newsletter,* October, 2009. https://loa-shared.s3.amazonaws.com /static/pdf/LOAStavansonBecomingAmericans.pdf.

Kellman, Steven G.. *The Translingual Imagination.* Lincoln: University of Nebraska Press, 2000.

Kellman, Steven G. "Writing South and North: Ariel Dorfman's Linguistic Ambidexterity." *Orbis Litterarum* 8, no. 3 (2013): 207–21.

Kharanauli, Besik. "Digging Out Potatoes." *The Common: A Modern Sense of Place.* Translated by Ilan Stavans and Gvantsa Jobava. May 11, 2018. https://www.thecommononline .org/tag/Gvantsa-Jobava/.

Leck, Sebastian. "Magazine Editor Quits after Outrage over Column Saying He Doesn't Believe in Cultural Appropriation." *National Post,* May 11, 2017. http://news.nationalpost .com/arts/magazine-editor-quits-after-writing-that-he-doesnt-believe-in-cultural -appropriation

Longoria, Eva. Speech to Democratic National Convention. Philadelphia, Pennsylvania, July 25, 2016. NBC News. https://www.youtube.com/watch?v=Kpc7g9GOJ8.

Maisonnat, Claude. "Le français dans l'écriture conradienne." *Cahiers victoriens et édouardiens* 78 (2013). https://cve.revues.org/959.

Manrique, Jaime. "A Man for All Seasons: A Bard's Vast and Lasting Legacy." *Washington Post,* October 19, 2003.

"Mean and Median Number of Books Read per Year, 2011–2015." Pew Research Center, August 31, 2016. http://www.pewinternet.org/2016/09/01/book-reading-2016/pi2016-09 -01book-readinga-02/.

Mendoza, Luis. "On Buffaloes, Body Snatching, and Bandidismo: Ilan Stavans's Appropriation of Oscar Acosta and the Chicano Experience. *Bilingual Review* 26, no. 1 (2001): 79–86.

Morson, Gary Paul. "The Intolerable Dream." *New Criterion* 34, no. 4 (2015): 9–13.

Nabokov, Vladimir. *Strong Opinions.* New York: Vintage, 1990.

Neruda, Pablo. *Selected Poems, By Pablo Neruda.* Edited by Ilan Stavans. New York: Farrar, Straus and Giroux, 2007.

"New York City Population." New York City Department of City Planning. http://www1.nyc
.gov/site/planning/data-maps/nyc-population/population-facts.page.

"New York Crime Rates 1960–2015." http://www.disastercenter.com/crime/nycrime.htm.

Newhouse, Alana. "Dissents Greets Isaac Bashevis Singer Bicentennial." *New York Times,*
June 17, 2004.

Pacheco, José Emilio. *Selected Poems.* Edited by George McWhirter. New York: New Directions, 1987.

Pagni, Andrea. "Review of *José Vasconcelos: The Prophet of Race.*" *Iberoamericana* 12, no. 48
(2012): 246–47.

Pakravan, Saïdeh. "A Writer in Exile: An Interview with Ilan Stavans." *Literary Review* 37,
no. 1 (1993): 43–55.

Paz, Octavio. *The Labyrinth of Solitude.* Translated by Lysander Kemp. New York: Grove,
1985.

Paz, Octavio. *The Monkey Grammarian.* Translated by Helen Lane. New York: Arcade, 1980.

Pew Research Center. "The Median American Reads Four Books per Year." http://www
.pewinternet.org/2016/09/01/book-reading-2016/pi2016–09–01book-readinga-01/.

Posner, Richard A. *Public Intellectuals: A Study of Decline: With a New Preface and Epilogue.*
Cambridge, MA: Harvard University Press, 2003.

Publishers Weekly. "Review of *A Most Imperfect Union.*" May 12, 2014. https://www.publishers
weekly.com/978-0-465-03669-1.

Randerson, James. "Childish Superstition: Einstein's Letter Makes View of Religion Relatively Clear." *The Guardian*, May 12, 2008. https://www.theguardian.com/science/2008
/may/12/peopleinscience.religion.

Restless Books Mission. http://www.restlessbooks.com/mission/.

The Restless Books Prize for Immigrant Writing. http://www.restlessbooks.com/prize
-for-new-immigrant-writing/.

Richardson, Lynda. "How to Be Both an Outsider and an Insider: 'The Czar of Latino
Literature and Culture' Finds Himself under Attack." *New York Times*, November 13,
1999.

Rivera, Tomás. . . . *y no se lo tragó la tierra.* Houston: Arte Publico, 1995.

Rosenbaum, Thane. "A Polyglot Pen." *New York Times Book Review*, September 16, 2001.

Sáez, Elena Machado. "Reconquista: Ilan Stavans and Multicultural Latino/a Discourse."
Latino Studies 7, no. 4 (2009): 410–34.

See, Carolyn. "Yo and Me." *Washington Post Book World*, August 24, 2001.

Sevilla, Maria Eugenia. "Desafia con Spanglish a puristas del idioma." *Palabra* (Saltillo),
June 26, 2002.

Shriver, Lionel. "Lionel Shriver's Full Speech: 'I Hope the Concept of Cultural Appropriation Is a Passing Fad.'" *The Guardian*, September 13, 2016. https://www.theguardian
.com/commentisfree/2016/sep/13/lionel-shrivers-full-speech-i-hope-the-concept-of
-cultural-appropriation-is-a-passing-fad.

Singer, Isaac Bashevis. *Collected Stories.* 3 vols. Edited by Ilan Stavans. New York: Library of America, 2004.

Singer, Isaac Bashevis. "Nobel Lecture." In *Nobel Lectures in Literature (1968–1980),* edited by Tore Frängsmyr and Sture Allen, 163–65. Singapore: World Scientific Publishing, 1993.

Sokol, Neal. *Ilan Stavans: Eight Conversations.* Madison: University of Wisconsin Press, 2004.

Solomon, Deborah. "The Way We Live Now: 11–02–03: Questions for Noam Chomsky; The Professorial Provocateur." *New York Times Magazine,* November 2, 2003. http://www .nytimes.com/2003/11/02/magazine/way-we-live-now-11–02–03-questions-for-noam -chomsky-professorial-provocateur.html.

Stavans, Ilan. "Adiós a la 'h.'" *New York Times,* March 2, 2018. https://www.nytimes.com /es/2018/03/02/opinion-stavans-adios-h-hache-espanol/.

Stavans, Ilan. Against Narrowness: Indie Publishing's Diversity Offers Response to Tyranny." *Foreword Reviews,* December 9, 2016. https://www.forewordreviews.com/articles /article/against-narrowness-indie-publishings-diversity-offers-response-to-tyranny/.

Stavans, Ilan. "Against the Ostrich Syndrome." *Academic Questions* 11, no. 1 (1997): 59–68.

Stavans, Ilan. " . . . and justice for all." *AGNI* 54 (2001): 357–60.

Stavans, Ilan. *Angelitos.* With art by Santiago Cohen. Columbus: Ohio State University Press, 2018.

Stavans, Ilan. *Antiheroes: Mexico and Its Detective Novel.* Translated by Jesse H. Lytle and Jennifer A. Matson. Madison, NJ: Fairleigh Dickinson University Press, 1997.

Stavans, Ilan. *Art and Anger: Essays on Politics and the Imagination.* Albuquerque: University of New Mexico Press, 1996.

Stavans, Ilan. *Bandido: Oscar "Zeta" Acosta and the Chicano Experience.* New York: HarperCollins, 1995.

Stavans, Ilan, ed. *Becoming Americans: Four Centuries of Immigrant Writing.* New York: Library of America, 2009.

Stavans, Ilan. *Borges, the Jew.* Albany: State University of New York Press, 2016.

Stavans, Ilan. *Cesar Chavez: A Photographic Essay.* El Paso, TX: Cinco Puntos Press, 2010.

Stavans, Ilan. *La condición hispánica.* Translated by Sergio M. Sarmiento. Mexico City: Fondo de Cultura Económica, Colección Tierra Firme, 1999. [Rayo/HarperCollins, 2001].

Stavans, Ilan. "Convocation." *Hopscotch: A Cultural Review* 1, no. 1 (1997): 2–3.

Stavans, Ilan. *A Critic's Journey.* Ann Arbor: University of Michigan Press, 2010.

Stavans, Ilan. *Días de diccionario.* Translated by Verónica Albin. Mexico: UNAM, 2006.

Stavans, Ilan. *Dictionary Days.* St. Paul, MN: Graywolf Press, 2005.

Stavans, Ilan. *The Disappearance.* Evanston, IL: Northwestern University Press, 2006.

Stavans, Ilan. "Disturbing Pablo Neruda's Rest." *New York Times,* April 9, 2013. https:// www.nytimes.com/2013/04/10/opinion/disturbing-pablo-nerudas-rest.html.

Stavans, Ilan. "Do All Chicanos Have an Inferiority Complex?" *Lingua Franca* blog. *Chronicle of Higher Education*, February 20, 2014. https://www.chronicle.com/blogs/lingua franca/2014/02/20/do-chicanos-have-an-inferiority-complex/.

Stavans, Ilan. "Dying in Hebrew." *Massachusetts Quarterly Review* 55, no. 4 (2016): 591–606.

Stavans, Ilan, ed. *Encyclopedia Latina*. 4 vols. New York: Grolier/Scholastic, 2005.

Stavans, Ilan. "Episode 24: The End of Representation—Junot Diaz." *In Contrast*. New England Public Radio. May 30, 2018. Podcast. https://cpa.ds.npr.org/wfcr/audio/2018/05 /incontrast24theendofrepresentation-junotdiazmp3?siteplayer=true&dl=1.

Stavans, Ilan. *The Essential Ilan Stavans*. New York: Routledge, 2000.

Stavans, Ilan. Foreword to *Chicano Movement for Beginners*, by Maceo Montoya, ix–xii. Danbury, CT: For Beginners, 2016.

Stavans, Ilan. Foreword to *My Sax Life: A Memoir*, by Paquito D'Rivera, vii–ix. Evanston, IL: Northwestern University Press, 2005.

Stavans, Ilan. Foreword to *Sal Si Puedes (Escape If You Can): Cesar Chavez and the New American Revolution*, by Peter Matthiessen, xxxvii–lii. Berkeley: University of California Press, 2014.

Stavans, Ilan. "Friday Takeaway: Forgetting." *Daily Hampshire Gazette*, June 15, 2018. http://www.gazettenet.com/friday-takeaway-18131898.

Stavans, Ilan. "Friday Takeway: Ilan Stavans on 'Despacito.'" *Daily Hampshire Gazette*, July 25, 2017. http://www.gazettenet.com/Friday-Takeaway-Ilan-Stavans-11639012.

Stavans, Ilan. "Friday Takeaway: On Aging." *Daily Hampshire Gazette*, July 16, 2017. http:// www.gazettenet.com/Friday-Takeway-On-Aging-11153376.

Stavans, Ilan. "Friday Takeaway: Teaching in the Age of Intolerance." *Daily Hampshire Gazette*, June 17, 2017. http://www.gazettenet.com/First-Person-10660157.

Stavans, Ilan, ed. *The FSG Book of Twentieth-Century Latin American Poetry*. New York: Farrar, Straus and Giroux, 2011.

Stavans, Ilan. *Gabriel García Márquez: Los años formativos, 1927–1970*. Translated by Juan Fernando Merino. Bogotá: Taurus/Historia, 2015.

Stavans, Ilan. *Gabriel García Márquez: The Early Years*. New York: Palgrave Macmillan, 2010.

Stavans, Ilan. "'Gangsta' Shakespeare." *Lingua Franca* blog. *Chronicle of Higher Education*, March 30, 2016. http://www.chronicle.com/blogs/linguafranca/2016/03/30/gangsta -shakespeare/.

Stavans, Ilan. "Globalism and Its Discontents: Point/Counterpoint." Amherst College. Course description. Fall 2018. https://www.amherst.edu/academiclife/departments /courses/1718F/COLQ/COLQ-411-1718F.

Stavans, Ilan. *God: A History*. Audiobook. Prince Frederick, MD: Recorded Books, 2014.

Stavans, Ilan. *Golemito*. Art by Teresa Villegas. Montgomery, AL: New South Books, 2013.

Stavans, Ilan. *The Hispanic Condition: Reflections on Culture and Identity in America*. New York: HarperCollins, 1995.

Stavans, Ilan. *I Love My Selfie*. With photography by Adál Alberto Maldonado. Durham, NC: Duke University Press, 2017.

Stavans, Ilan, ed. *The Ilan Stavans Reader*. New York: Routledge, 2000.

Stavans, Ilan. *Imagining Columbus: The Literary Voyage*. New York: Twayne, 1993.

Stavans, Ilan. Introduction to *Backlands: The Canudos Campaign*, by Euclides da Cunha, translated by Elizabeth Lowe, vii–xxiv. New York: Penguin, 2010.

Stavans, Ilan. Introduction to *Barrio Boy: 40th Anniversary Edition*, by Ernesto Galarza, ix–xxiii. Notre Dame, IN: University of Notre Dame Press, 2011.

Stavans, Ilan. Introduction to *The Book of Memories*, by Ana María Shua, translated by Dick Gerdes, ix–xiii. Albuquerque: University of New Mexico Press, 1998.

Stavans, Ilan. Introduction to *Chronicle of the Narváez Expedition*, by Álvar Núñez Cabeza de Vaca, translated by Fanny Bandelier. New York: Penguin, 2002.

Stavans, Ilan. Introduction to *Facundo: Or, Civilization and Barbarism*, by Domingo F. Sarmiento, translated by Mary Mann, vii–xxxii. New York: Penguin, 1998.

Stavans, Ilan. Introduction to *Hopscotch, Blow-up and Other Stories, We Love Glenda So Much and Other Tales*, by Julio Cortázar, translated by Gregory Rabassa and Paul Blackburn, vii–xv. New York: Knopf, 2014.

Stavans, Ilan. Introduction to *The Martyr: Luis de Carvajal, A Secret Jew in Sixteenth-Century Mexico*, by Martin A. Cohen, xix–xxiv. Albuquerque, NM: University of New Mexico Press, 2001.

Stavans, Ilan. Introduction to *The Monkey Grammarian*, by Octavio Paz, translated by Helen Lane. New York: Arcade, 2017.

Stavans, Ilan. Introduction to *Poems, Protest, and a Dream: Selected Writings: Sor Juana Inés de la Cruz*, by Sor Juana Inés de la Cruz, translated by Margaret Sayers Peden, xi–xliv. New York: Penguin: 1997.

Stavans, Ilan. *The Inveterate Dreamer: Essays & Conversations on Jewish Culture*. Lincoln, NE: University of Nebraska Press, 2001.

Stavans, Ilan. "Is American Literature Parochial?" *World Literature Today*, July, 2013. https://www.worldliteraturetoday.org/2013/july/american-literature-parochial-ilan -stavans.

Stavans, Ilan, ed. *Isaac Bashevis Singer: An Album*. New York: Library of America, 2004.

Stavans, Ilan. *José Vasconcelos: The Prophet of Race*. New Brunswick, NJ: Rutgers University Press, 2011.

Stavans, Ilan. *Knowledge and Censorship*. With Verónica Albin. New York: Palgrave Macmillan, 2008.

Stavans, Ilan. "The Languages of the World Cup." *Lingua Franca* blog. *Chronicle of Higher Education*, July 14, 2014. http://www.chronicle.com/blogs/linguafranca/2014/07/14/the -languages-of-the-world-cup-2/.

Stavans, Ilan, ed. *Latina Writers*. Westport, CT: Greenwood, 2008.

Stavans, Ilan. *Latino USA: A Cartoon History*. New York: Basic Books, 2000.

Stavans, Ilan. *Latinos in the United States: What Everyone Needs to Know.* New York: Oxford University Press, 2018.

Stavans, Ilan, ed. *Lengua Fresca: Latinos Writing on the Edge.* Boston: Houghton Mifflin, 2006.

Stavans, Ilan. ¡*Lotería!* Art by Teresa Villegas. With an essay and riddles by Ilan Stavans. Tucson: University of Arizona Press, 2003.

Stavans, Ilan. *Love & Language.* New Haven, CT: Yale University Press, 2007.

Stavans, Ilan, ed. *A Luis Leal Reader.* Evanston, IL: Northwestern University Press, 2007.

Stavans, Ilan (as Ilán Stavchansky). "Mexico y su novela policial." PhD diss. Columbia University, 1990.

Stavans, Ilan. *A Most Imperfect Union: A Contrarian History of the United States.* With art by Lalo Alcaraz. New York: Basic Books, 2014.

Stavans, Ilan. *Mr. Spic Goes to Washington.* Illustrated by Roberto Weil. Berkeley, CA: Soft Skull Press, 2008.

Stavans, Ilan, ed. *Mutual Impressions: Writers from the Americas Reading One Another.* Raleigh, NC: Duke University Press, 1999.

Stavans, Ilan. *New World Haggadah.* With art by Gloria Abella Ballen. Santa Fe, NM: Gaon Books, 2016.

Stavans, Ilan, ed. *The Norton Anthology of Latino Literature.* New York: Norton, 2011.

Stavans, Ilan. *The Novel That Invented Modernity: Don Quixote.* Audiobook. Prince Frederick, MD: Recorded Books, 2014.

Stavans, Ilan. "Now More Than Ever." Restless Books Blog. http://www.restlessbooks .com/blog/2016/11/10/now-more-than-ever.

Stavans, Ilan. *Octavio Paz: A Meditation.* Tucson: University of Arizona Press, 2001.

Stavans, Ilan. *On Borrowed Words: A Memoir of Language.* New York: Penguin, 2001.

Stavans, Ilan. "On Self-Translation." *Los Angeles Review of Books*, August 23, 2016. https:// lareviewofbooks.org/article/on-self-translation/#!.

Stavans, Ilan. *On Self-Translation: Meditations on Language.* Albany: State University of New York Press, 2018.

Stavans, Ilan. "On Separate Ground." In *Passion, Memory, and Identity*, edited by Marjorie Agosin, 1–16. Albuquerque: University of New Mexico Press, 1999.

Stavans, Ilan. *Once@9:53am: A Fotonovela.* With photography by Marcelo Brodsky. Buenos Aires: Asunto Impreso, 2011.

Stavans, Ilan. *The One-Handed Pianist and Other Stories.* Evanston, IL: Northwestern University Press, 2007.

Stavans, Ilan. "Our Dreams." *Tikkun*, May 3, 2016. http://www.tikkun.org/tikkundaily/2016 /05/03/our-dreams/.

Stavans, Ilan. *The Oven: An Anti-Lecture.* Amherst: University of Massachusetts Press, 2018.

Stavans, Ilan, ed. *The Oxford Book of Jewish Stories.* New York: Oxford University Press, 1998.

Stavans, Ilan, ed. *The Oxford Book of Latin American Essays*. New York: Oxford University Press, 1997.

Stavans, Ilan, ed. *Oy, Caramba! An Anthology of Jewish Stories from Latin America*. Albuquerque: University of New Mexico Press, 2016.

Stavans, Ilan. *Palabras prestadas: Autobiografía*. Translated by Leticia Barrera. Santiago: Fondo de Cultura Económica, 2013.

Stavans, Ilan. "Philip Roth's New Novel about Philip Roth." *The Forward*, March 13, 2009.

Stavans, Ilan. *La pianista manca*. Caracas: Alfadil Ediciones, 1991.

Stavans, Ilan. Preface to *I Explain a Few Things: Selected Poems*, by Pablo Neruda, edited by Ilan Stavans, xiii–xx. New York: Farrar, Straus and Giroux, 2007.

Stavans, Ilan. "A Professor's Inner Journey." *Chronicle of Higher Education*, February 21, 2016.

Stavans, Ilan. *Prontuario*. Mexico City: Joaquín Mortiz, 1992.

Stavans, Ilan. *Quijote: La novela y el mundo*. Translated by Juan Fernando Merino. Bogotá: Semana Libros, 2015.

Stavans, Ilan. *Quixote: The Novel and the World*. New York: Norton, 2015.

Stavans, Ilan. *Resurrecting Hebrew*. New York: Schocken, 2008.

Stavans, Ilan. *Return to Centro Histórico: A Mexican Jew Looks for His Roots*. New Brunswick, NJ: Rutgers University Press, 2012.

Stavans, Ilan. *The Riddle of Cantínflas: Essays on Hispanic Popular Culture*. Albuquerque: University of New Mexico Press, 1998.

Stavans, Ilan, ed. *The Schocken Book of Modern Sephardic Literature*. New York: Schocken, 2005.

Stavans, Ilan, ed. *The Scroll and the Cross: 1,000 Years of Jewish-Hispanic Literature*. New York: Routledge, 2003.

Stavans, Ilan. *Singer's Typewriter and Mine: Reflections on Jewish Culture*. Lincoln: University of Nebraska Press, 2012.

Stavans, Ilan. "¿Son necesarios los dos signos de exclamación?" *New York Times*, May 12, 2018. https://www.nytimes.com/es/2018/05/12/opinion-stavans-signo-exclamacion-espanol/.

Stavans, Ilan. *Sor Juana: Or, the Persistence of Pop*. Tucson: University of Arizona Press, 2018.

Stavans, Ilan. *Spanglish: The Making of a New American Language*. New York: HarperCollins, 2003.

Stavans, Ilan. "Sublime Goal, Philosophical Narrator: World Cup Broadcaster Andrés Cantor Predicts the Future." *Chronicle of Higher Education*, June 18, 2018. https://www.chronicle.com/blogs/linguafranca/2018/06/18/sublime-goal-philosophical-narrator-world-cup-broadcaster-andres-cantor-predicts-the-future/.

Stavans, Ilan. *Talia y el cielo: o el libro de los ensueños*. Mexico City: Plaza y Valdes Editores, 1989.

Stavans, Ilan, ed. *Tropical Synagogues: Short Stories by Jewish-Latin American Writers*. New York: Holmes and Meier, 1994.

Stavans, Ilan. "Trump Point/Counterpoint." Amherst College. Course description. Fall 2017. https://www.amherst.edu/academiclife/departments/courses/1718F/COLQ /COLQ-411-1718F.

Stavans, Ilan. "Trump, the Wall and the Spanish Language." *New York Times*, January 30, 2017. https://www.nytimes.com/2017/01/30/opinion/trump-the-wall-and-the-spanish -language.html?r=0.

Stavans, Ilan. Twitter account. https://twitter.com/IlanStavans.

Stavans, Ilan. *The United States of Mestizo*. Montgomery, AL: NewSouth Books, 2013.

Stavans, Ilan. *The Wall*. Pittsburgh: University of Pittsburgh Press, 2018.

Stavans, Ilan. *With All Thine Heart: Love and the Bible*. With Mordecai Drache. New Brunswick, NJ: Rutgers University Press, 2010.

Stavans, Ilan. *Words in Transit: Stories of Immigrants*. Springfield: University of Massachusetts Press, 2016.

Stavans, Ilan, and Frederick Luis Aldama. *¡Muy Pop!: Conversations on Latino Popular Culture*. Ann Arbor: University of Michigan Press, 2013.

Stavans, Ilan, and Harold Augenbraum, eds. *Growing Up Latino: Memoirs and Stories*. Boston: Houghton Mifflin, 1993.

Stavans, Ilan, and Justin David. "God as an Idea." *Massachusetts Review*. Blog, January 27, 2015. http://www.massreview.org/node/404.

Stavans, Ilan, and Joshua Ellison. *Reclaiming Travel*. Durham, NC: Duke University Press, 2015.

Stavans, Ilan, and Carlos Fonseca. "All Writing Is a Kind of Exile: Ilan Stavans and Carlos Fonseca in Conversation." *Literary Hub*, December 12, 2016. http://lithub.com/all -writing-is-a-kind-of-exile/.

Stavans, Ilan, and Marie-Lise Gazarian Gautier. "The Man with a Thousand Masks: An Interview with Ilan Stavans." *Confluencia* 10, no. 1 (1994): 141–51.

Stavans, Ilan, and Jorge J. E. Gracia. *Thirteen Ways of Looking at Latino Art*. Durham, NC: Duke University Press, 2014.

Stavans, Ilan, and Iván Jakšić. *What Is La Hispanidad? A Conversation*. Austin: University of Texas Press, 2011.

Stavans, Ilan, and Lisa Newman. Interview. Yiddish Book Center. Email newsletter, June 17, 2018. https://mail.google.com/mail/u/0/?tab=wm#search/Ilan+Stavans+French /FMfcgxvwzcHJVLNqTzjZzhzwLVxJkX.

Stavans, Ilan, and Max Page. "On Jealousy: A Conversation between Ilan Stavans and Max Page." *Los Angeles Review of Books*, March 10, 2018. https://lareviewofbooks.org/article /on-jealousy-a-conversation-between-ilan-stavans-and-max-page/#!.

Stavans, Ilan, and Steve Sheinkin. *El Iluminado: A Graphic Novel*. New York: Basic Books, 2012.

Stavans, Ilan, and Juan Villoro. *El oja en la nuca.* Barcelona: Anagrama, 2014.

Stavans, Ilan, and Donald Yates. "A Mode of Truth: A Conversation between Ilan Stavans and Donald Yates." *Michigan Quarterly Review* 48, no. 4 (Fall 2009): 589–606.

Stavans, Ilan, and Raúl Zurita. *Saber morir: conversaciones.* Santiago de Chile: Ediciones Universidad Diego Portales, 2014.

Stevens-Arroyo, Anthony M. "Latino Thinkers, up North—The Hispanic Condition: Reflections on Culture and Identity in America by Ilan Stevens." [sic] *Commonweal* 122, no. 15 (1995): 22.

Swanson, Philip. "Review of *Antiheroes: Mexico and Its Detective Novel.*" *Modern Language Review* 93, no. 4 (1998): 1143–44.

Swift, Jonathan. *The Prose Works of Jonathan Swift, Vol. 1: A Tale of a Tub, The Battle of the Books and Other Early Works.* Edited by Temple Scott. New York: AMS Press, 1971.

Temes, Peter S. "In Short." *New York Times Book Review,* May 21, 1995.

Tobar, Hector. "Ilan Stavans' New Polyglot Project: Multilingual E-book Publishing." *Los Angeles Times,* November 11, 2013. http://www.latimes.com/books/jacketcopy/la-et-jc-ilan-stavans-new-polyglot-project-multilingual-ebook-publishing-20131111-story.html.

Tomkins, Calvin. "Troubling Pictures." *New Yorker,* April 10, 2017, 30–35.

Valencia Assogna, Leonardo. "Review of *La condición hispanica.*" *Dispositio: Crítica Cultural en Latinoamérica: Paradigmas globales y enunicaciones locales* 24, no. 5 (1999): 211–13.

Wassner, Dalia. "Mexican Jewish? A Conversation with Ilan Stavans." *Journal of Modern Jewish Studies* 15, no. 3 (2016): 491–503.

Weber, Bruce. "Juan Gelman, Argentine Poet of the Left, Dies at 83." *New York Times,* January 22, 2014.

Weinberger, Eliot. "Paz as 'Dictator.'" *Transition* 63 (1994): 120–25.

Weinreich, Max. *History of the Yiddish Language.* Vol 2, edited by Paul Glasser, translated by Shlomo Noble. New Haven, CT: Yale University Press, 2008.

Wilson, Edmund. *An Edmund Wilson Celebration.* Edited by John Wain. Oxford: Phaidon, 1978.

Wilson, Edmund. "The Fruits of the MLA: I. 'Their Wedding Journey.'" *New York Review of Books,* September 26, 1968.

Wilson, Edmund. "The Fruits of the MLA: II. Mark Twain." *New York Review of Books,* October 10, 1968.

Ybarra-Frausto, Tomás. "Rasquachismo, a Chicano Sensibility." In *Chicano Aesthetics: Rasquachismo,* edited by Rudy Guglielmo, Tomás Ybarra-Frausto, and Lennee Eller, 5–8. Exhibition catalog. Phoenix, AZ: MARS/Movimiento Artistico del Río Salado, 1989.

Yeats, W. B. *Autobiographies.* Edited by William H. O'Donnell and Douglas N. Archibald. New York: Scribner, 1999.

Zinn, Howard. *A People's History of the United States.* New York: HarperCollins, 1980.

Zong, Jie, and Jeanne Batalova. "Frequently Requested Statistics on Immigrants and Immigration in the United States." Migration Policy Institute, March 8, 2017. http://www.migrationpolicy.org/article/frequently-requested-statistics-immigrants-and-immigration-united-states.

INDEX